COLLINS COUNTRYSIDE SERIES
INSECT LIFE

In the same series

LIFE ON THE SEA SHORE *John Barrett*

BIRDS *Christopher Perrins*

WOODLANDS *William Condry*

PLANTLIFE *C. T. Prime*

ROCKS *David Dineley*

These books are intended to offer the beginner a modern introduction to British natural history. Written by experienced field workers who are also successful teachers, they assume no previous training and are carefully illustrated. It is hoped that they will help to spread understanding and love of our wild plant and animal life, and the desire to conserve it for the future.

COLLINS COUNTRYSIDE SERIES

INSECT LIFE

*

Michael Tweedie

Line drawings by
DENYS OVENDEN

COLLINS
ST JAMES'S PLACE, LONDON

William Collins Sons & Co Ltd
London · Glasgow · Sydney · Auckland
Toronto · Johannesburg

First published 1977
© Michael Tweedie 1977
ISBN 0 00 219343 4
Filmset by Jolly & Barber Ltd., Rugby
Made and Printed in Great Britain by
William Collins Sons & Co Ltd Glasgow

CONTENTS

5

PHOTOGRAPHS

All photographs are by the author

PREFACE

THERE is widespread awareness of the threat to wild life all over the world, but most of the recognition in this context goes to the mammals and birds. Few nature reserves are established specially for insects and commercial exploitation of them meets with only limited protest. The destruction by pesticides and other means of thousands of harmless (or even beneficial) insects for every one noxious one passes practically unnoticed.

The fact is that conservation is largely a matter of sentiment. But with the whole of the beauty and diversity of life on the earth at risk the time has come for such sentiment to be applied without narrow preference and prejudice.

Our warm-blooded vertebrate relatives are easier to understand and appreciate than insects, whose evolutionary pedigree is so very remote from our own. Perhaps the insects' way of life can never be fully understood, but any sincere effort to do so will lead at least to some sympathy with them, and to an appreciation that in diversity they excel all other animals and at least equal them in beauty, and are just as well worth saving. I have written this book with the hope constantly in mind that it may help naturalists who are not entomologists to see more clearly the insects' place in the world. If it captures the attention of some who are not yet naturalists I shall be even better rewarded.

CHAPTER I

INTRODUCING INSECTS

WHAT THEY ARE

To many people an insect is any small creature that buzzes or flutters around or scuttles about on an indeterminate number of legs. It is unfortunate that the word 'arthropod' was not accepted into common speech instead of 'insect', for this image fits the arthropods quite well but fails to give a satisfactory definition of the insects as they are defined by zoologists, and as we must regard them here.

The Arthropoda is the name of a major division or Phylum of the Animal Kingdom. The word means 'jointed legs' (arthritis is an affliction of the joints), and describes the legs of these animals, which are formed of rings or tube-like segments of more or less rigid material articulated so that the segments can pivot on each other. The body is also formed of a series of segments, basically similar to each other but variously adapted, some of them moveable by articulation with the ones in front and behind, some fused together. These also normally have a tough and rigid covering, and this, together with that of the limbs, serves both as a suit of armour and as a skeleton. Both body and limbs contain muscles which are attached to them inside, just as our muscles are attached to the

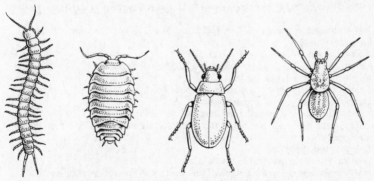

Centipede, woodlouse, beetle and spider are all arthropods, but only the beetle is an insect.

11

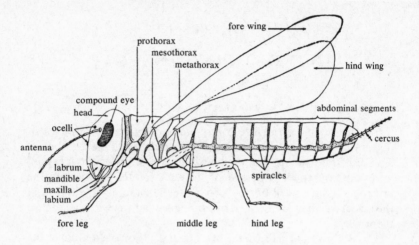

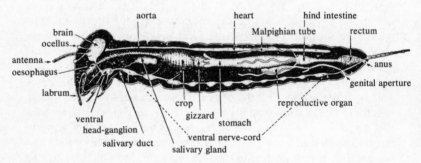

STRUCTURE OF AN INSECT. (From A. D. Imms *Insect Natural History*, Collins)

Key to the diagrams above. Obvious terms like 'head', 'fore wing', 'hind leg' are not defined.

Aorta, the main dorsal blood vessel.

Cercus, a jointed appendage on the last abdominal segment.

Coxa, the basal joint of the leg.

Femur, the 'thigh' or main proximal joint of the leg.

Galea, the outer lobe of the maxilla.

Labial palp, a small jointed appendage of the labium.

Labium, the lower lip, formed of the fused second maxillae of more primitive arthropods.

Labrum, the upper lip.

Lacinia, the inner lobe of the maxilla.

Malpighian tube, one of a bundle of fine tubes serving as organs of excretion.

Mandibles, the front pair of jaws, used for biting.

Maxillae, the first maxillae of more primitive arthropods, used as jaws for manipulating the food.

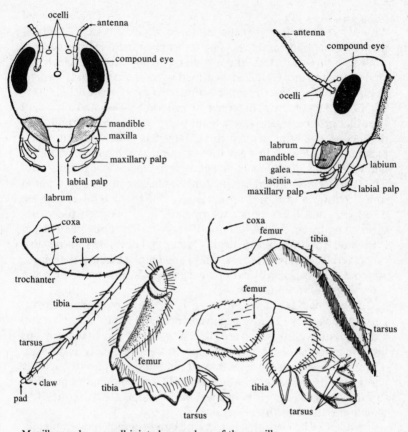

Maxillary palp, a small jointed appendage of the maxilla.

Mesothorax, the middle segment of the thorax.

Metathorax, the hind segment of the thorax.

Ocelli, simple eyes, as distinct from the compound eye.

Oesophagus, the gullet.

Prothorax, the front segment of the thorax.

Salivary gland and duct, the system supplying liquid, usually digestive in function, to the mouthparts.

Spiracles, external openings of the tracheal breathing system.

Tarsus, the foot, articulated to the tibia and usually consisting of several joints.

Tibia, the shin or shank of the leg, articulated to the femur.

Trochanter, a small intermediate part of the leg between the coxa and the femur.

Ventral head ganglion, nerve centre in lower part of head, connected on each side by nerves to the brain or dorsal head ganglion.

Ventral nerve cord, the connected series of nerve centres or ganglia forming the central nervous system.

outer surface of our bones. Contraction of the muscles combined with pivoting or flexing at the joints, provides a system of movements for the body and legs. The arthropods include crustaceans, such as crabs, lobsters and woodlice, arachnids, of which the spiders are the most familiar, centipedes, millipedes – and insects.

Insects differ from the other arthropods most obviously in having three pairs of legs. No typical arthropod has less and almost all the other groups or Classes have more; spiders have four pairs and millipedes sometimes over three hundred. The segments that make up their legs follow a plan something like that of a vertebrate animal's limbs, and they have been given names in a similar way. The terms *femur* (thigh), *tibia* (shin) and *tarsus* (foot) are common to vertebrate and insect terminology, but there is of course no developmental correspondence or homology between the structures so named in the two groups of animals. The body of an insect is divided into three parts, head, thorax and abdomen (terms also borrowed from vertebrate anatomy) and many insects have wings, which are possessed by no other arthropods, nor indeed by any other invertebrate animals.

On the head of an insect there is a single pair of antennae, carrying a variety of sense organs, simple and compound eyes and a set of mouth-parts which are laterally symmetrical in the way our limbs are, so that the jaws work sideways not vertically as ours do. The mouth-parts comprise a pair of mandibles, a pair of maxillae and a lower lip or labium, which is really a second pair of maxillae fused together; both pairs of maxillae are separate in centipedes, which are allied to the ancestors of insects.

It must now be clear that insects are constructed on a completely different plan from the familiar vertebrate animals such as lizards and birds, mice and men, and cannot be described and discussed with any precision without the use of special terms. Some of these have been introduced in connection with the limbs and mouth-parts and there are a few more referring to various parts of the body. All those which we shall use are explained in the diagrams and key on pages 12 and 13.

The internal anatomy can be summarized briefly. The central nervous system is ventral in position and the long tubular heart or aorta is dorsal. The stomach and gut run in the normal way from mouth to anus, and some insects have the anterior part of it modified for storing or for grinding up food, and terms like 'crop' and 'gizzard' are used to describe this. The part just behind the mouth and concerned in swallowing is the pharynx. The excretory function that we associate with the kidneys is performed by a bundle of fine tubes, the Malpighian tubules, attached to the hind part of the gut or intestine. The internal reproductive organs, ovaries and testes, lie in the cavity of the abdomen. The blood is not confined in narrow blood vessels but is merely pumped through large spaces or sinuses in the body cavity, bathing the various organs as it circulates, taking up nutriment from the intestine and enabling the Malpighian tubules to absorb from it the products of excretion. The blood is not concerned with carrying oxygen to the organs or tissues in the manner familiar in vertebrate animals.

HOW THEY BREATHE

This brings us to the very remarkable system by which insects breathe. Respiration is effected by internal tubes called tracheae which convey oxygen to the tissues, branching repeatedly over and among the various organs. In land-living insects the tubes communicate with the atmosphere through pairs of spiracles, which are easily seen on each side of the body segments of a caterpillar, and are present on the thorax and abdomen of mature insects. The passage of air into and out of the spiracles is usually regulated by some sort of closing mechanism or valve. The tracheal tubes are kept open by spiral thickening in their walls, and as they branch they become progressively finer until they can only be seen with a microscope. In the larger and more active insects parts of them are dilated to form air sacs. When these are present the insect performs rhythmic pumping movements with the abdomen, which expand and collapse the air sacs and force air into and out of them. This breathing action can be seen clearly by closely inspecting a wasp or a bee. In small insects, and in the innermost and finest tracheal tubes of the larger ones, gaseous diffusion is the means by which oxygen is brought to the tissues and carbon dioxide conveyed away from them.

Although insects are so numerous and successful very few of them are bigger than a mouse. Their mode of respiration is believed to be the chief reason for this limitation in size. The combination of not very efficient 'breathing' and gaseous diffusion is not adequate to convey oxygen along progressively narrower tracheae for a distance of more than about one cm. An insect with a body diameter of two cm. is already encountering difficulty in aerating its innermost organs and tissues. Most of the largest insects, such as the 26cm. long giant stick insect *(Pharnacia)* have attenuated bodies, so that none of their internal organs are more than a few millimetres from the surface. This must also have been true of the gigantic extinct dragonflies of the Carboniferous Period, whose wing-span was nearly 70 cm.

CHITIN AND SCLEROTIN

The external covering of insects is known as the cuticle and has as its basis a tough fibrous substance called chitin, consisting chemically of the nitrogen-containing sugar glucosamine. Of itself chitin forms the flexible skin of the joints and the soft skin of the body of caterpillars and other rapidly growing larvae. In all the parts that are stiffened or hardened, including the body covering, limbs and wings of most adult insects, protein is combined with the chitin and it undergoes a chemical process rather like the tanning of hides to make leather. The horny substance so produced is called sclerotin; very thin membranes of it are transparent but thicker structures are brown or black. The hard shell of a beetle is a heavily sclerotized structure, and how strong and hard it can be is well illustrated by the jaws of some of the wood-boring beetle larvae, which can bite through sheets of copper or zinc.

Whether it is of sclerotin or chitin the cuticle of an insect is covered with a very thin waxy layer called the epicuticle, which makes the insect's body perfectly waterproof. This is of great importance in the success story of the insects, not because it keeps water out but because it prevents loss of water from the body fluids. Woodlice, which are crustaceans and lack this waxy outer covering, quickly die in a dry atmosphere; but insects are found everywhere, flying high in the air and living in deserts where loss of water is the greatest threat to life of all kinds.

The sclerotized cuticle provides not only a coat of armour as effective as the calcareous shell of a crab, and waterproof in addition, but both serve as a skeleton as well. This was mentioned earlier as a feature of the arthropods, but an external skeleton is in such curious contrast to our internal skeleton of bone that we must examine its advantages and disadvantages more closely.

A typical arthropod limb consists of a jointed system of hollow rigid cylinders. Muscles can work just as well attached to the inside of a cylinder as to the outside of a rod, like a vertebrate limb-bone,

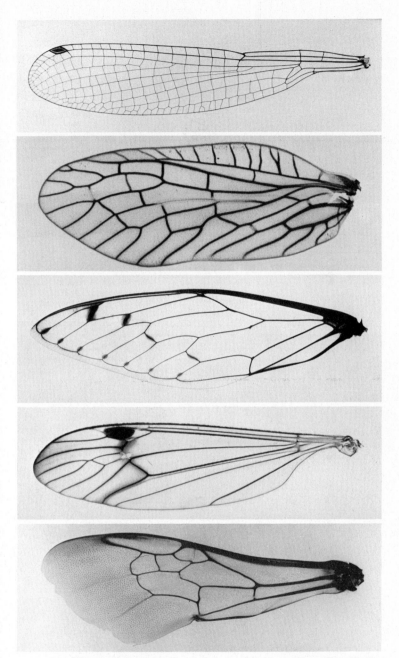

PLATE I. **Wings of insects.** *From top to bottom*: damselfly (Order Odonata); alder-fly (Neuroptera); cicada (Hemiptera); crane-fly (Diptera); bumblebee (Hymenoptera). The first two are relatively primitive, the others more advanced types.

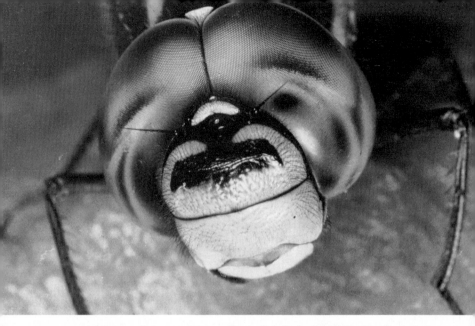

PLATE 2. **Compound eyes.** *Above*, head of a dragonfly (*Aeshna*); *below*, of a horse-fly (*Tabanus*).

and the cylinder is mechanically more efficient. Given the same proportions of rigid material to muscle, a cylinder containing the muscle will be much more resistant to breaking strains than a rod surrounded by muscle. In addition the external skeleton of an insect protects it against injury from the outside and against desiccation. But it has one serious disadvantage: since it is not surrounded by living tissue it cannot change its size and form, allowing the animal to grow. As a consequence of this all arthropods are constantly growing out of their skins, until they reach maturity, rather as a schoolboy grows out of his clothes. The boy's clothes can be passed on to his protesting younger brother, and many arthropods frugally eat their shed skins, but some wastage of material is unavoidable. Also this process of moulting or ecdysis is almost always a hazardous one, as it imposes a period of inactivity on the animal whenever it occurs, and the covering of a hard-shelled arthropod is soft and vulnerable for a short time after ecdysis has taken place. Growth can proceed immediately after ecdysis because the new covering is wrinkled as well as soft, but insects constituted to endure hard times do not necessarily grow. The larva of the carpet beetle *(Dermestes)* can stand months of starvation, during which it continues to shed its skin, growing *smaller* at each moult.

WALKING AND JUMPING

Insects use their legs for crawling, walking or jumping. None have more than the three pairs of the jointed legs to which the word 'arthropod' refers, but the larvae of butterflies and moths and of sawflies have pairs of unjointed clasper-like 'feet' on the abdominal segments. In the sawflies these number six to eight and in most Lepidoptera there are five pairs. In crawling the fore part of the body and the true legs are extended and each pair of claspers is moved forward in series, the hindmost ones last. Repetition of this action, with appropriate waves of contraction and elongation passing along the body, result in forward movement. In the 'woolly

An ordinary moth caterpillar (*above*) with five pairs of false legs or claspers, and a Geometrid or 'looper' caterpillar in two positions to show the method of walking.

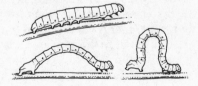

bear' caterpillars of tiger and ermine moths this can be so rapid that they appear to be running rather than crawling. In the larvae of the Geometrid moths (which include the well known peppered and magpie moths) only the two hindmost claspers are present, and these caterpillars progress by bending the body into a vertical loop by releasing the hold of the claspers and bringing them to a point close behind the true legs; these then release their hold and the body is extended forwards. The looping mode of progression has given its name to this Family of moths, the Geometridae or 'earth-measurers'.

The movement of insects like beetles that run on six legs is basically simple. The first and third feet on one side and the middle foot on the other are planted on the ground, so that the insect is supported on a tripod. A backward push by these three legs carries the body forward and at the same time the other three are moved forward and planted to repeat the motion. An insect walking slowly conforms fairly well to this pattern of progression, but in rapid running complicated variations are imposed on the simple sequence of forward shifting tripods.

A cardinal beetle (*Pyrochroa*) running. In the upper figure the left fore and hind legs and the right middle leg are on the ground, the others are raised and moving forwards; the reverse in the lower figure. Drawn from eletronic flash photographs.

Some insects such as fleas and grasshoppers make prodigious jumps by means of the enlarged hind legs. Their small size enables them to leap many times their own length without any remarkable output of energy, and to land without injury. Arithmetical comparison between the jump of a flea and its equivalent performed by a man is quite unrealistic and not worth making. Nevertheless the jump of the flea was a problem for a long time because it could not be explained in terms of the known properties of muscle and the flea's anatomy. Muscle simply could not contract fast enough to provide the necessary energy in the available time. High speed photography showed that when a flea is about to jump it gathers its legs up on either side, waits for a fraction of a second and then makes its powerful and incredibly rapid kick, throwing itself upwards and forwards. Microdissection reveals that fleas have a pad of an extremely elastic substance surrounding the articulation between two rigid sclerotized structures in the thorax called the notum and pleuron. The gathering up of the hind legs bends the elastic pad and so stores energy in it. Sudden release of the mechanism makes all the stored energy available in a very brief space of time and so provides high speed power for the jump. The elastic substance is called resilin, and it is more elastic than any artificial substance; if it, or something equally good, could be synthesized this would be of value in engineering and balls could be made to bounce higher than ever before.

Locusts are on the lower limit of size for an animal to jump by direct muscular contraction; smaller jumping insects probably all have some sort of energy storing mechanism.

The principle of energy storing can be illustrated by comparing the performance of a javelin thrower and an archer. The former throws his spear by direct action of his muscles. The archer, using a comparable amount of muscular power, draws his bowstring back, storing energy in the bent bow. The release of the string gives the arrow far greater velocity and range than that of the javelin. A child playing with a pogo stick uses energy stored in the compressed spring to make repeated jumps.

WINGS AND FLIGHT

Almost all kinds of arthropods run but only the insects can fly, and we know from the fossil record that they learned to fly in the evolutionary sense, long before any other group of animals. The earliest fossils of winged insects date from the Upper Carboniferous Period, the time when most of the world's coal was formed, about 300 million years ago. There were cockroaches at that time and primitive kinds of mayflies and dragonflies; some of the latter were the largest insects known to have existed.

Typically insects have two pairs of wings, and these are not modified limbs, as are those of birds, bats and the extinct pterodactyls. Study of fossils and of primitive living insects suggests that they arose from lateral expansions of the thoracic segments, which have been called *paranota*. In the extinct and very primitive cockroach-like insects called Palaeodictyoptera the second and third thoracic segments bore wings, as in modern insects, and the first segment a pair of paranota. Although there is no direct fossil evidence it seems likely that the even more primitive wingless ancestors of these ancient insects had paranota on all three thoracic segments, and that some of these took to jumping. This led to the paranota becoming enlarged to form gliding planes, and later those of the hinder two thoracic segments became articulated and under muscular control and developed into wings. The silverfish *(Lepisma)*, a wingless and primitive modern insect, has paranota on the thorax, and they contain tracheae whose arrangement recalls that in the structures that represent the wings in the early stages of growth of winged insects.

An insect's wing consists of two very thin and often transparent layers of sclerotin. When it is fully formed these are closely adherent and appear as a single sheet, just as a flattened paper bag does. The wing is strengthened by a framework of hollow rods of sclerotin, which are usually called the veins and their arrangement in the wing is termed the venation. They do play the part of blood-vessels during development of the wing, and to some extent when it is fully formed, but their main function is to support the membranous sclerotin of which the wing consists.

The arrangement of veins in the wing is far from being a haphazard network. On the contrary it is virtually constant for each species, and the different Orders (and smaller taxonomic groups as well) usually show characters in the venation that are of importance in classification. One reason why the wing venation is such a valuable feature in classification is that the wings of insects are often found in a good state of preservation as fossils. In very fine-grained sediments flattened imprints of wings can give a clear and complete picture of the venation, so that its evolution can be studied in detail in living insects and through the relevant part of the geological record as well.

Studies of this kind have led to a hypothetical primitive wing type in which the longitudinal veins are given names or numbers. In all the Orders of winged insects the venation can be related more or less closely with the primitive model and the same names used for veins which appear to be homologous, just as the same system of naming can be applied to the bones in the fore-limb of a man, a bat and a crocodile. Their uniformity of structure implies that all the land vertebrates are descendants of one ancestral group of amphibians, and in the same way it can be inferred that wings have been developed by insects only once in their evolutionary history. In the early winged insects of the fossil record the longitudinal veins are joined by a close network of cross-veins, and this primitive condition is seen in the modern mayflies and dragonflies. The tendency in evolution has been towards reduction in the number of the veins, especially the cross-veins, and strengthening of those that remain, particularly those at and near the front margin of the wing. The result is to stiffen the front edge of the wing, which is the part that bears the greatest stress in flight. The wings of some of the larger flies and bees illustrate this condition.

In most insects with rapid and well controlled flight there is either only one pair of wings, as in flies, or the two pairs are coupled together in some way so that they work in unison. In bees and wasps there is a row of minute hooks along the front edge of the hind-wing which engage in a fold on the rear edge of the fore-wing. In butterflies and some moths the wings overlap, fore over hind, so that the down stroke, powered mainly by the forewing, is applied to both simultaneously. Many moths have a wing-coupling apparatus which is different in the two sexes. The male has a bristle, the *frenulum*, near the base of the hind-wing, which is held by a hook-shaped *retinaculum* on the lower surface of the fore-wing. In females the frenulum usually consists of a number of bristles and the retinaculum of a tuft of hairs or scales in which the bristles are anchored.

Insect flight is more like that of a helicopter than of an aeroplane because both propulsion and lift are produced by the movement of the wings rather than by the air flow resulting from forward movement. The main difference is of course that the wings of an insect oscillate with an up-and-down motion instead of rotating. In simple terms an insect's wings work by beating up and down and at the same time twisting at the base in such a way that the hind edge rises above the costa or leading edge on the down stroke and falls below it on the up stroke. The effect is to fan a stream of air downwards and backwards, propelling the insect forward and supporting it against the pull of gravity.

The way in which power and control are applied to the wings tells an interesting story of increasing complexity from what are

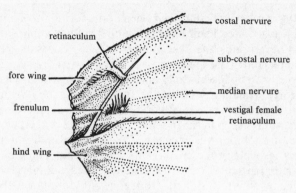

MALE UNDERSIDE

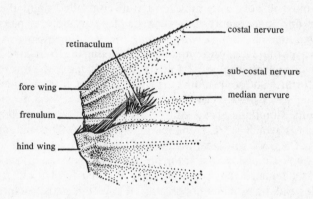

FEMALE UNDERSIDE

The apparatus which unites the fore and hind wings of a moth during flight. (From E. B. Ford *Butterflies*, Collins.)

regarded on general grounds as primitive insects to the more recently evolved and highly organized groups. In each of the two thoracic segments that bear wings there are three sets of flight muscles, the direct, indirect and accessory muscles. The direct flight muscles are fairly simple in their action and are the main source of power in dragonflies, the Orthoptera (grasshoppers, locusts, crickets), the Dictyoptera (cockroaches and mantises) and also in beetles. All but the last are primitive, and beetles can be said to have made less of a speciality of flying than most of the other

Diagrams to show the action of (*left*) direct flight muscles and (*right*) indirect flight muscles.

'higher' insects. These muscles act in the way shown above. The wing pivots at a point very close to its base and the muscles are attached to the wing base at points close to the pivot and on each side of it. Contraction of the inner muscles pulls the base down and swings the wings up, while the outer muscles pull the wing down when they contract.

The wings of flies, bees, wasps, moths and indeed of most flying insects are powered in a quite different way by indirect flight muscles. In the simplified form illustrated there is a vertical pair of these muscles, and a longitudinal pair which are seen in cross-section. They are not attached to the wings at all, but to the walls of the thorax, and the wings are moved up and down by rapid raising and lowering of its dorsal wall. When the vertical muscles contract this is pulled down and the wings move upwards; when the longitudinal muscles contract the top of the thorax is arched and pushed up and the wings beat downwards. The actual anatomical details of the action of both the direct and indirect systems are enormously more complicated than those shown in the diagrams. When the power is applied indirectly, direct muscles may be present to twist the bases of the wings and so provide the angle of attack on the air that is required for whatever manoeuvre the insect is performing. Also there are numerous accessory muscles that brace the walls of the thorax against the stresses imposed on them by the powerful flight muscles, and control complex elastic mechanisms in certain parts of the thorax.

One of these is the so-called 'click-mechanism', which has been closely studied in flies and also exists in some other insects. When this is present the indirect muscles do not merely push the wing up and down as they alternately contract and relax. The wings are held in their up and down positions by minute locks or catches, which are not released until deformation of the elastic walls of the thorax reaches a certain degree of tension. This build-up and sudden release of tension causes the wings to move with a snapping motion which gives increased speed and efficiency to their strokes. The working is rather like that of a spring-operated electric switch, and it involves energy storage by structures made of resilin similar in principle to that described in the case of the jumping flea.

Large insects such as dragonflies and locusts, lacking the click mechanism, beat their wings at fairly low frequencies, around 20 up-and-down strokes a second. In these the muscles are controlled by separate impulses from the central nervous system. In normal flight the beats are synchronized and identical on both sides, but dragonflies can operate each of the four wings independently, and high-speed photographs of them may show the fore-wings right up and the hind-wings right down, so that end-on the insect looks like a capital X. In evolutionary terms the flight of dragonflies is crude and old-fashioned, but they are, surprisingly, masters of speed and manoeuverability.

In small insects, possessing the click mechanism, frequencies are much higher. Bees and flies beat their wings about 200 times a second, mosquitoes up to 600, and the astonishing frequency of 1,000 per second has been recorded for a minute biting midge called *Forcipomyia*. Wing beats at this rate could not possibly be controlled by a separate motor nerve-impulse for each beat. The explanation is that the flight muscles of such insects are of a special type called fibrillar muscle, which has the property of contracting as a direct response to being stretched. The vertical and longitudinal indirect muscles form antagonistic sets, that is to say one set will be stretched when the other reaches its limit of contraction. The response of the stretched muscle to contract, and then to relax at the finish of the wing-beat it has actuated, is immediate, so that repeated cycles of contraction, relaxation and extension or stretching are set up. In small insects, in which the distances travelled by the moving parts are minute, these cycles can operate at fantastic speed and the whole process is as automatic as an internal combustion engine, and quite independent of nerve impulses, other than those which start it and stop it. The twisting of the wing bases that accompanies flight is no longer under muscular control, but is brought about by further elaboration of their articulation to the thorax.

Calculation, based on aeronautical principles, is said to prove that a bumblebee, with its large body and rather small wings, cannot fly. The fact that it can fly quite efficiently is due to the wonderful perfection of the mechanism by which the wings are actuated.

The flight of the two-winged flies or Diptera is controlled and assisted by a pair of remarkable organs called halteres, which are in fact highly modified hind-wings. They have the form of short knobbed rods, and during flight they vibrate up and down at the same rate as the wings. Their speed of vibration is such that they acquire the same sort of self-stability as a gyroscope, so that if the flying insect is tipped or inclined a strain is set up at the base of each haltere. This is detected by sense organs in the cuticle which transmit nervous impulses enabling the insect to control its position in flight. A blowfly deprived of its halteres flies wildly and crashes to the ground, but, oddly enough, a cotton thread attached to the tip of its abdomen acts like the tail of a kite and to some extent restores the mutilated fly's stability.

Insect flight is efficient but it consumes a great deal of energy. A blowfly, which uses carbohydrate as fuel to provide power for its wings, may consume as much as 35 per cent of its weight in an hour's flying. Locusts, which store their energy in the form of fat, 'burn' less than one per cent of their body weight in an hour. In general insects which undertake long migratory flights, such as locusts, butterflies and moths, use stored fat as a source of energy. This is the source of the 'grease' that sometimes distresses collectors by spreading over the body and wings of preserved specimens of butterflies and moths.

The actual speed of flight of insects is difficult to measure as they can seldom be observed flying in a straight line over a determined distance. The fact is that insects do not fly very fast. Bees and butterflies fly at 10–15 km/h and horse-flies have been observed following vehicles (presumably taking them for large mammals) at between 40 and 50 km/h. The maximum speed of a large Australian dragonfly was estimated at 58 km/h. Big hawk-moths like the convolvulus hawk, and some even larger tropical species, have very powerful indirect flight muscles and also their fore and hind-wings are coupled together in a way that almost certainly promotes efficiency and speed of flight. It may well be that they are the swiftest of all insects, but as they are only active at night observation of their flight is very difficult.

INSECT BURROWERS

Burrowing underground could be regarded as the antithesis of flight. Many kinds of larvae are burrowers with little in the way of special adaptation beyond an elongate shape. The mole cricket, however, is a professional and almost swims through the soil. Its fore-legs are flattened and spined and very powerful, and move outwards and backwards almost exactly like those of a mole. A mole cricket held in your hand will try to force its way out between your fingers, and its efforts are too painful for any ordinary person to endure.

SENSES AND SENSE ORGANS

It is convenient to think of insects feeling, smelling, seeing and hearing their way about the world just as we do, but a more accurate way of putting it is to say that they react to the same sort of stimuli. We have no idea what sort of sensations an insect experiences, but its sense organs are so different from ours that their sensations and ours probably have very little in common.

The sense organs lie in the cuticle, and at the base of each one there is a sense cell, or group of such cells, connected by nerves to the central nervous system. With every moult all the chitinous or sclerotized parts of the sense organs are discarded with the cast-off cuticle and new structures grow from the cells in the new cuticle. The new structures may be more complex than the old, leading to the fully developed organ in the adult insect. In highly developed insects an entirely new set of sense organs appears with last ecdysis or moult.

The simplest sense organs that insects possess are tiny bristles or hairs which may arise anywhere on the body and appendages. Each one has a ball-and-socket joint at its base and any movement of the hair pivots this joint and stimulates the nerve, so that these provide the insect with a sense of touch. They are usually scattered over the body and limbs but are most numerous on the antennae, and ground-living insects like earwigs and cockroaches can be seen to explore constantly the surface ahead of them with their antennae as they move. Sensory hairs are also numerous on the tail appendages or cerci of some primitive insects such as may-flies and stone-flies and the very primitive bristle-tails. Presumably they serve as collectors of information from behind the insect just as the antennae do in front of it.

The hairs are also moved by, and sensitive to, air currents, and some of those on the face and antennae may provide the stimulus to start and maintain flight. A locust that is suspended or fixed will beat its wings as if in flight if a current of air is directed on it from the front, but if the sensory hairs are covered with cellulose paint it makes no response to the current of air, nor can it be persuaded to fly if released.

Sound is another sort of air movement. It consists of compression waves whose frequency varies over the whole range that we can hear and extends into frequencies too low to be audible to us, or too high, subsonic and ultrasonic waves. Many insects detect such waves by means of their sensory hairs, probably without much discrimination or true 'hearing'; caterpillars react to sounds by flinching or throwing up their heads, and they have no organs specially adapted for hearing.

Not all the minute and simple sense organs scattered over the insect's cuticle are activated by hairs. Some have the form of little pegs or hardly project at all, and others are embedded in the cuticle. These last are called chordotonal organs and are sensitive to minute stresses tending to bend or stretch the cuticle. Even in the dark we know whether we are holding our arms at our side or above our head. Tension in our muscles and tendons tells us, but insects rely for such information largely on chordotonal organs and on patches of tactile hairs at the limb joints or around the neck and 'waist' where the thorax articulates with the head in front and the abdomen behind. For perception of the direction of gravity, and for maintaining our balance, we rely on movements of liquid in the semicircular canals associated with our inner ear. In almost all insects this sense is external, depending on perception of contact and pressure between the parts of the body, perceived by hairs or by chordotonal organs embedded in the cuticle. The water scorpion *(Nepa)* has been shown to maintain itself on an even keel under water not by direct reference to gravity but to the water pressure. If it tilts over mechanical sense organs near its spiracles on each side inform the insect that one side of it is deeper than the other and it automatically corrects its position. The aquatic bug *Aphelocheirus* lives in rather deep water, sometimes over six metres, and has similar organs which react to absolute hydrostatic pressure and tell the bug how deep it is.

Hearing and 'ears'

I have mentioned the rudimentary sense of hearing provided by sensory hairs. Many insects have more elaborate hearing organs, which are curiously diverse both in structure and situation. Almost all insects have a group of chordotonal organs near the base of each antenna, which are sensitive to any change in the antenna's position. These groups have been given the name Johnston's organ, and in the midges and mosquitoes it is elaborated to form an organ of hearing, sensitive but with a narrowly limited scope. It is particularly developed in the males, which have the antennae profusely branched and feathered. It appears that the male antennae of each species have a definite resonant frequency so that they vibrate in response to sound transmitted at this frequency. In each species it corresponds exactly to the speed of the wing beat of the female of the same species, that of the male himself being always faster. In the case of a female with a wing beat of, say, 300 beats per second, any male of her species whose Johnston's organ informs him that his antennae are vibrating knows that a prospective mate is nearby and flies towards her; his own wing beats and those of other males, or of either sex of different species, simply fail to register. Male mosquitoes will assemble on a tuning fork vibrating at the critical frequency for their species, or even fly into the open mouth of a singer who strikes and holds the right note.

Grasshoppers, crickets and cicadas, which communicate by sound, have more specialized organs of hearing, though these

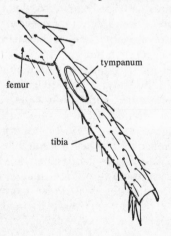

femur

tympanum

tibia

Tibia and base of femur of the fore-leg of a cricket, showing the hearing organ.

again are adapted to react only to the particular pattern of sound made by the voice of their own species. Here there is a membrane or *tympanum* in the cuticle which vibrates in response to airborne sound, and which is attached to numerous chordotonal organs beneath it. These ear-drums are most often situated near the waist on each side, on the last segment of the thorax or the foremost part of the abdomen. This is their situation in cicadas and in the short-horned grasshoppers and locusts. In the crickets and bush-crickets the ears have the form of a tympanum in a tiny pocket or slit in the tibia of each fore-leg. The bush-cricket *Tettigonia* has been observed 'scanning' its surroundings by swinging the fore-legs.

Many night-flying moths possess tympana on the thorax or abdomen but have no sort of voice at all. It has been shown that they are sensitive only to ultrasonic frequencies within the range of those emitted by hunting bats, and it appears certain that these organs are an adaptation for protection against these very important predators of moths. Bats give out brief pulses of sound at a pitch of 30,000-80,000 cycles per second, quite inaudible to us, and they use the reflected echoes of these pulses both to detect and avoid obstructions in the dark and to locate and hunt their prey in flight. When moths that possess tympana are exposed to pursuit by bats, or to artificial ultrasonic sounds, they fly wildly or drop to the ground.

Smelling and tasting

The chemical senses of taste and smell cannot really be separated either in men or insects, though it is convenient to speak of tasting substances dissolved in liquid and smelling them when they are suspended in vapour. In aquatic animals, insects and fish alike, the distinction breaks down altogether. Organs associated with either taste or smell are called chemo-receptors.

Insects certainly taste their food with their mouthparts and will reject it if it is unpleasantly flavoured, for example with salt or quinine. Bees and plant-sucking bugs have chemoreceptors at the base of the proboscis or in the mouth, and in insects with less highly adapted mouthparts, such as cockroaches and beetles, the maxillary and labial palps carry taste organs. A frequent and rather unexpected site for insect organs of taste is in the tarsi or feet of the fore-legs. Many kinds of flies and butterflies immediately extend the proboscis if the tarsi come into contact with sweetened water.

Experiment with a red admiral butterfly showed that it can distinguish between distilled water and a solution of sucrose equal to the weakest solution detectable by the human tongue diluted a further 200 times.

A minute wasp called *Trichogramma*, which lays its eggs inside the eggs of other insects, will not lay in an egg which has already received an egg from another *Trichogramma*. Normally traces of the wasp's anticipator on the host egg give her enough information, but if already parasitised eggs are carefully washed she will start the action of laying, inserting her ovipositor, and then withdraw it. Here is an insect having exceedingly sensitive chemoreceptors at the tip of her tail; since they respond to the liquid contents of the egg they are organs of taste rather than smell.

The sense of smell of insects is located mainly on the antennae. The last eight segments of a bee's antennae bear large numbers of minute chemoreceptors, plate-like in surface view, the 'plate' consisting of extremely thin cuticle. Bees, of course, identify flowers by their scent as well as by their colours, both features of the flowers being functionally addressed to insects which will visit them in search of nectar and pollinate them. Scarab beetles hold their antennae aloft when searching for dung to eat and lay their eggs in.

Many insects secrete substances called pheromones by means of which they communicate with each other. The most important of these are highly volatile and are released by the female insect to attract the male. The majority of moths find their mates in this way and collectors sometimes obtain male specimens by exposing a newly emerged female in a cage and capturing her eager suitors, a method known as 'assembling'. In the emperors and giant silk-moths (Saturniidae) the females are rather sluggish and the males very active fliers, and the males also have elaborately branched or 'plumose' antennae. When the males of a Chinese species, *Actias selene*, were released 11 kilometres from caged females a quarter of them found their way to the cage, and distances of two miles and

Head of a male Saturnid moth, showing the elaborately plumose antennae. (From A. D. Imms *Insect Natural History*, Collins.)

more have been reported for other species. The plumose antennae of the male are undoubtedly adapted to detect the scent molecules in some way, but it is difficult to understand how even such organs as these can be relied upon to intercept a scent as widely dispersed as that of the female pheromone must be at such distances.

Experiments made with the gypsy moth *(Lymantria dispar)* in America have a bearing on this problem. The female pheromone of the moth was extracted and analysed and found to have the chemical composition of a fairly simple alcohol. Very dilute solutions of it were made in petroleum ether and tests were carried out on male moths by dipping a glass rod in the solution and bringing it near the moth's antennae. If he responded by vibrating his wings the test was regarded as positive. The most dilute solution to give a positive test was 10^{-10} microgram of the pheromone dissolved in a cubic centimetre of petroleum ether. This figure represents one ten thousand million millionth part of a gram, the amount present on the glass rod being quite a small fraction even of this. Clearly only a few molecules of the pheromone need alight on the antennae for the presence of the female to be detected. It seems that the scent organs are wholly specialized to detect this one substance, as the male moth shows no sign of being able to perceive any other odour. He does not need to use his sense of smell to search for food, as moths of this family, the Lymantridae, never feed in the adult or imago stage. The same is true of the Saturniidae, another Family noted for the great sensitivity of the males to the female pheromone.

EYES AND SIGHT

The light receptive organs of insects can fairly be called eyes as they are always situated on the head. They are of two kinds, ocelli or simple eyes and compound or faceted eyes; in an ocellus there is a single lens, in a compound eye many. Two kinds of ocelli are recognized, those found in the larvae of insects with distinct larva and pupa stages, and those of adult insects. The former are on the sides of the head and are the only eyes that the larva has. There may be one on each side, as in sawfly larvae, or a group; caterpillars of butterflies and moths usually have six. They can detect movement of objects, and larvae which orientate themselves to the direction of the light cease to do so if their ocelli are covered with paint. In most adult winged insects there is, in addition to a pair of compound eyes, a triangular group of three ocelli on the top of the head. Their presence is puzzling as there seems to be nothing they can do that the compound eyes cannot do better. Experiments have been made which appear to show that insects make less good use of their compound eyes if the ocelli are painted over, and they may play some part in maintaining the tone and sensitivity of the optic nervous system. In its simplest form an ocellus consists of a biconvex lens at the surface of the cuticle with a transparent corneagen layer beneath it. Below this layer are the light-sensitive cells grouped in little bundles called retinulae.

The compound eyes, which are the visual organs of most adult insects, are much more complicated. The whole eye has an external transparent layer called the cornea divided up into facets, usually hexagonal in form, each of which is the outermost part of a visual structure called an ommatidium. In some dragonflies there are over 20,000 ommatidia in each eye, and most of the higher insects like flies and butterflies have several thousand. In worker ants there may be a dozen or less, and the eye hardly functions as a compound organ.

The ommatidium has the form of a long, narrow cone tapering towards its inner end, and they are all in contact with each other. The eye therefore consists of a bundle of very numerous precisely arranged radiating ommatidia. Each one has a small hexagon of transparent cornea on the outside with a corneagen layer under it. Below this is a group of four transparent cone cells which may be

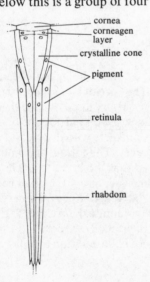

cornea
corneagen layer
crystalline cone
pigment
retinula
rhabdom

Diagram of a single unit or ommatidium of the compound eye of an insect.

PLATE 3. **Ultraviolet 'coloration' of flowers;** photos on the left taken in white light, those on the right in ultraviolet light. *From top to bottom*, silverweed (*Potentilla anserina*); evening primrose (*Oenothera* sp.); common fleabane (*Pulicaria dysenterica*).

PLATE 4. *Above*, male and female of the gatekeeper butterfly (*Pyronia tithonus*) showing the dark coloured band of scent scales (androconia) on the fore-wing of the male; *below*, male (*left*) and female of the glow-worm beetle (*Lampyris noctiluca*).

solid, the so-called crystalline cone, or may contain liquid. Under the narrow ends of the cone cells is a long central rod, the rhabdom, surrounded by a bundle of elongated visual cells (usually seven) that comprise the retinula. Light is focused by the cornea and cone cells onto the outer end of the rhabdom-retinula bundle. Although an image is formed by this combination of lenses, it seems that the insect appreciates not this image but the amount of light collected by the ommatidium. Their precise radial arrangement ensures that every point in the visual field is directionally covered by an ommatidium in the same way as an astronomer's telescope covers a small portion of the night sky. Light intensity coming from the surroundings is thus resolved into an even pattern of points and an image is formed on the same principle as in half-tone printing, in which evenly spaced black dots of different sizes determine all tones between black and white. (Examine one of the plates in this book with a strong lens.) Just as a finer 'screen' gives greater detail in printing, so very numerous ommatidia can be supposed to provide better appreciation of images. Dragonflies, which pursue flying prey, hunting by sight, require and have the most highly developed compound eyes.

There is an interesting additional specialization. In the eyes of day-flying insects the cones and retinulae are surrounded by layers of black pigment which isolates each ommatidium optically from its neighbours. In insects that fly at night this pigment is absent so that light 'leaks' through from one ommatidium to the next. It can be supposed that the former arrangement gives better image formation, but that much of the available light is absorbed by the pigment and visually wasted. When the pigment is absent the insect will resolve images less clearly but will have better night vision. Some insects, including the nocturnal moths, have it both ways. In the dark the ommatidia permit the passage of light from one to another, but bright light causes pigment to move up between the ommatidia forming isolating sheaths like those of the daylight type of eye.

THE MOTH AND THE CANDLE

Nocturnal insects are well known to fly to a bright source of light, and moth collectors take advantage of this by setting traps whose lure is a light bulb, preferably one emitting a lot of ultra-violet light to which moths are particularly sensitive. They do not fly to the light because it 'attracts' them, as the smell of food or of the sex pheromone of their own species does. The explanation of the fatal allure of the candle for the moth involves the insect's reaction to fixed natural lights, the sun and moon and perhaps bright stars. Such a light will be received by a small group of ommatidia in a certain part of the eye; the reflex behaviour is to keep the same part illuminated so that, if the light is a distant one, the moth will continue in a straight line until diverted by some other stimulus. If, however, the light is close by, its direction relative to a straight line of flight will change rapidly and the moth's attempt to keep the same eye facets illuminated will lead to its flying in a curve that develops into a spiral converging on the source of light.

It seems likely that even at its best the compound eye produces nothing like the detailed image seen by ourselves and other vertebrate animals. Possibly, however, movement in their surroundings is more readily perceived by insects. Those who have stalked butterflies and dragonflies in order to capture or photograph them are likely to subscribe to this view.

Some insects certainly have colour vision. Honey-bees have been trained to associate certain colours with the presence of food, and such experiments have revealed that they can distinguish between four 'colours' or bands in the light spectrum. They correspond to what we see as blue-violet, as blue-green and as red, yellow and green, the last being seen by the bees as one colour. The fourth is in the ultra-violet and so invisible to us. Both bees and butterflies use their colour vision to recognize flowers, and butterflies to recognize members of their own species in courtship.

The compound eye has one capacity that is totally lacking in our own unaided vision: it is able to distinguish polarized light, that is light whose vibration is restricted to one plane. The light reflected to the earth from the sky is partly polarized, the proportion being least towards the sun and in the opposite direction and greatest in a ring or 'equator' mid-way between these two directions. As the sun's position moves across the sky this pattern of polarization moves with it, so that ability to see it provides a capacity to use the sun as a compass even on a cloudy day, provided a certain amount of blue sky is visible. The fact that insects do use the direction of the sun's radiation as a compass can be shown by altering its direction with a mirror or a prism. A running ant subjected to this treatment will respond by turning through an angle equivalent to that through which the light has been diverted.

Bees certainly use this light compass, both in full sunlight and with sky partly obscured, in navigating on their long foraging journeys to and from the hive. Since a bee may be away an hour or more it must have a time sense in order to make allowance for the sun's movement during its absence. It is now known that bees possess a 'physiological clock' that works on a 24-hour basis. Not only do they navigate in a way that requires a sense of time, but they work to a time table. After being fed with syrup for several days at a fixed time they will appear at the feeding table at that time and not earlier or later, with a very small margin of error. Normally bees start to forage soon after sunrise. A colony flown across the Atlantic from Europe continued to commence their day's work by reference to their own physiological clock, quite out of phase with the hours of light and darkness in America, and it took them some time to adjust themselves to the new succession of night and day.

In a different kind of experiment a cockroach is imprisoned in a sort of cage in which its activity is automatically and continuously recorded. The most usual type is a drum which revolves like a treadmill when the insect inside it walks or runs, and remains still when it is at rest. When it is subjected to 24-hour day and night determined by switching on and off of artificial light, it has an activity rhythm of exactly 24 hours. If, however, it is kept for a fairly long period in continual darkness its activity continues to show a rhythm that is almost but usually not quite the same. It may be a little slower, say 24½ hours, and this continues quite regularly until, after ten days, it is 'getting up' and 'going to bed' five hours late.

This sort of time-keeping that runs a little fast or slow is very general in insects and other animals as well, and does not matter much because the regular alternation of night and day is always available in nature to apply the necessary correction. The biological rhythm is called 'circadian' from the Latin *circa diem:* 'about a day'. Almost all animals that have been investigated seem to have an internal clock of this type. It is developed in man, but is so suppressed by the use of mechanical time keepers that we cannot now rely on it. The business man's 'jet-lag' is really his physiological clock reminding him that he has upset the routine which it imposes on his body.

CHAPTER 2

HOW THEY LIVE

NUMBERS AND DIVERSITY

THE human population of the world is now approaching 4,000 millions, far greater than that of any other animal species of comparable size. It has more than doubled during the last hundred years and its rapid increase is a matter of concern to everyone who has any regard for the future of humanity. We are, of course, relatively gigantic animals; the vast majority of species are smaller than men and all insects very much smaller, so their populations can be enormously larger. It is hardly possible to think in terms of the global populations of common and widely distributed insects like the house-fly. The inhabitants of a single large ants' or termites' nest may number several millions, and the nests of some of the more abundant species would certainly number millions if counted over large areas. Abnormal proliferation or 'population explosion' sometimes occurs among insects, and those of the notorious big grasshoppers called locusts can produce terrible devastation. A big swarm of the desert locust (*Schistocerca gregaria*) may cover a hundred square kilometres and, with each locust weighing two to three grams, the total weight of such a swarm has been estimated at 70,000 tons.

Estimates of this kind are arrived at by counting samples, as large as time and other circumstances will allow them to be, applying some method of measurement to ascertain the proportion of your sample to the whole, and then using the two sets of figures as a basis for calculation. It is the second stage in this progression that is the least reliable in taking a census of myriads of scurrying ants, or of a huge, widely dispersed mass of hungry locusts, constantly moving on as the green landscape turns brown behind them. More accurate estimates can be obtained of the astonishingly large numbers of tiny insects and other arthropods that inhabit the shallow layers of the soil.

The method is simple in principle: a square metre of soil, to a depth of 20 or 30 cm., is taken from, say, an area of grassland and all the living arthropods are extracted from it and counted. It is best to think of the operation in terms of arthropods as no method of extraction can separate insects from other members of the Phylum, and the minute arachnids called mites often predominate numerically even over insects. The operation is repeated several times with widely separated samples within the area, to obtain an average figure, and the number per hectare arrived at by calculation. Here the difficulty is in completely and thoroughly extracting all the living insects and other fauna.

The earliest piece of apparatus to be designed for research of this kind was the well-known Berlese funnel. This consists of a large funnel held vertically in a stand with its spout over the receptacle that is to receive the insects. Half-way down the body of the funnel is a horizontal partition of wire mesh or any other sort of screen that will allow small animals through and support the sample of soil that is put on top of it. When the freshly collected soil is in place heat is applied above the funnel; an electric light bulb hung a few inches over it is as good as anything. The heating and drying of the soil drives the arthropods downwards until they come to the screen, and eventually they drop through this into the receptacle. The Berlese funnel is an excellent instrument for getting a general idea of the arthropod fauna present in a sample of soil or leaf-litter, or an old bird's nest, but for quantitative work it is unsatisfactory because many of the small and relatively inactive creatures in the upper part of the sample will die from heat and desiccation before they reach the screen. Various refinements have been applied to the Berlese funnel, but for obtaining realistic information about the numbers of minute arthropods living in the soil it was long ago superseded by the flotation method.

For this the soil is first gently but thoroughly disintegrated until it consists of particles so fine that no arthropod, however minute, can hide or be trapped inside one of them. Freezing to $-12°c.$ and then thawing is one way of doing this, or chemical reagents may be used. The muddy suspension is put into a cylinder filled with liquid to which more is added from below, so that it continually overflows. The animals, being lighter, are carried up into the overflow while the soil particles sink. The overflow is then directed through a series of sieves of increasingly fine mesh which sort the animals out by size. Salt water is used because its higher density floats the animals up more effectively. After this mechanical separation benzene is added and forms a floating layer at the surface. This separates arthropods from vegetable debris because their cuticle is wetted by the benzene so that they pass into the layer, while the vegetable matter remains at the interface between the benzene and the water.

Using these and other refinements Professor Salt, working at Cambridge in 1943, found that an acre of English pasture which he investigated harboured over a thousand million arthropods, of which the majority, 666 million, were mites. The most abundant insects were springtails, numbering 248 million; bristle-tails, bugs and beetles amounted to 116 million and other arthropods such as centipedes and millipedes to about 38 million. Farm soil in Iowa in the USA, has been found to contain up to 100 million springtails *per square metre*, but this probably represents a peak population rather than a normal condition.

Nearly a million species

Insects occur not only in enormous numbers but in astonishing diversity. Rather less than a million species have already been described and named, and several thousand new species are found and described every year. Estimates of the total of existing species range from about twice the number that are known to five million. At least five-sixths of the known animals in the world are insects. One thing that is certain is that a good proportion of the insects now inhabiting the earth will never be known to us, for we shall unwittingly exterminate them before any specimens are collected and described. This process has been going on now for a long time with the destruction of the flora of oceanic islands by felling trees and introducing goats and other voracious herbivores. Many of the plant species become extinct, with their dependent insects, and even when a pitiful remnant of a plant species survives in places inaccessible even to goats, the insects associated with it are likely to have disappeared. Most of such insects and plants are endemics that have evolved in isolation and exist nowhere else. Felling of forest on the continents and greater islands must already have wiped out some localized species, and the process appears to be accelerating with horrifying speed.

Specific diversity gives scope for the wonderful range in size, form and colour that we see among insects. The most massive of them are the African Goliath beetles, and measurements reveal that they have a bulk eight million times that of the smallest beetles; the smallest mammal, the Etruscan shrew, which weighs about two grams has a quarter-millionth the mass of a five-ton elephant.

Standing near an illuminated sheet near tropical forest, to which moths are flying in hundreds, one feels after a time that every possible permutation of form and colour has appeared. And then a moth settles on the sheet so completely different from any seen before that the eye picks it up the instant it arrives. Museum collections of butterflies can be joyously inspected, drawer after drawer, but after a time the viewer's sense of wonder becomes blunted and then stupefied by too much diversity and beauty. Some beetles are gorgeous or fantastic, but the majority look to the lay eye simply like larger or smaller beetles, or not like beetles at all; many are too small to be seen clearly without magnification. Some 275,000 species are known; even in Britain there are 3,700 and almost every year one or two beetles are added to the British fauna, occasionally a new species, more usually ones that are already known from other lands with a similar climate.

Insects are everywhere

That is enough, perhaps more than enough, of figures illustrating insect numbers and diversity. Ubiquity is an obvious concomitant of those figures: insects can be expected, and are found on land, in every possible situation in which one would look for living creatures and in some where one would not. On the other hand very few insects have invaded the sea. Those that have done so only skate on its surface or live between tide marks. This may well be due to the fact that another group of arthropods, the Crustacea, got there first. When insects evolved as pioneer land animals some 400 million years ago the crustaceans were already the dominant small animals of the sea, just as they are today. They fill every marine niche that an arthropod can occupy and have never been successfully challenged by any other group of the jointed-legged animals. It could be said that they are the most versatile arthropods, for insects and crustaceans share the inland fresh waters, and woodlice and some tropical crabs are well adapted for life on dry land in humid conditions, though all the crabs must return to water to breed.

As I discuss various aspects of insect biology we shall encounter them in most of their normal environments, but it is worth turning aside to take a look at one curious Family of flies which seem to break several of the rules that determine where it is possible for an animal to live. These are the Brine-flies, Family Ephydridae, so called because the larvae of some of them live in salt water near the sea. The common British species *Ephydra riparia* is one of these, but in the Mono Lake in California *Ephydra hyans* breeds in water almost as salt as that of the Dead Sea, and is the only aquatic insect known from the lake. In Iceland another Ephydrid, *Scatella thermarum*, is found breeding in water at 48° C, too hot to put your hand into. These flies pass their lives on the carpet of green algae which floats at the surface, feeding on the algae and laying their eggs on it. The larvae live below the surface, also feeding on the algae. Since the hot water contains no oxygen their mode of respiration was a puzzle to biologists until it was found that they obtain this, as well as their food, from the algae, absorbing through their skins the oxygen given off by the plant in the course of photosynthesis. Most extraordinary of the Ephydrids is the petroleum fly, *Psilopa petrolei*, another denizen of California. Its larva lives in pools of crude oil that seep out of the ground in the oil fields, and the species is known only from this locality. Both the cuticle and the lining of the intestine are adapted to protect the living tissues and organs from the oil, which permanently fills the larva's gut as well as surrounding its body. Both this and the other Californian species obtain their food from the bodies of the insects that fall into the oil or brine and drown.

COURTSHIP AND MATING

Sexual reproduction is the rule among insects, as it is among all higher animals and plants, though it is not invariable. Usually the male insect seeks out the female, using his sense of smell, hearing or sight to locate her. Examples of the first two have been given in Chapter 1, the mosquito flying to sound having the musical pitch of the female's wing-beat, and the extraordinary effectiveness of the pheromone of female moths in attracting males from great distances. It is probable that the majority of insects seek and recognize members of their own species, in order to mate, by the use of chemoreceptors. This must be true of the great hordes that live on and below the surface of the soil, in leaf litter and in thick grass or foliage. Most of them are small or minute and are difficult to observe because they are only at ease and likely to behave naturally when they are hidden from view. Also our own sense of smell is so defective that we can very seldom have any direct appreciation of olfactory communication between insects, whereas we can frequently observe their visual or auditory signals as clearly as they can themselves.

In many day-flying insects recognition is obviously visual, and the bright patterns of butterflies' wings have been evolved largely and perhaps mainly for this purpose. They are not as a rule very discriminating, at any rate at long range: a resting butterfly will often fly to intercept another of a similar species or a male of his own. Final recognition at close quarters seems to depend on reception of scent by one or both partners.

A German entomologist, Dr. Dietrich Magnus, has made a series of ingenious experiments on the silver-washed fritillary (*Argynnis paphia*) using a piece of apparatus that has come to be known as the butterfly merry-go-round. This consisted of a boom four metres long which was made to rotate horizontally on a pivot at its centre. At each end was an upright rod to the top of which a model butterfly could be attached, and a fluttering motion was mechanically imparted to the model when the boom rotated. It was established previously that at close range objects smeared with the pheromone of the female fritillary excited the males, but they flew freely to a variety of the moving models, only breaking away when close enough to discover that the dummy lacked the female scent. Details of the results were interesting. The shape of the moving dummy made little difference; the males flew as readily to fluttering triangles or discs as to carefully made butterfly models. The tawny orange colour was important, but not the pattern of black spots, in fact models were more attractive without them. Size was important, but not 'correct' size; dummies smaller than the female fritillary were not very attractive, but larger ones, up to four times the right size, were progressively more so. The fluttering, producing an alternation of orange and dark colour, was of great importance, in fact a rotating spool with alternating bands of black and orange attracted the male butterflies, and the faster it rotated the better they liked it, up to a speed of 75 black and orange alternations a second, much faster than a female fritillary can beat its wings. The female visual image most exciting to the males was a butterfly four times their own size, plain orange in colour and beating its wings at unnaturally high speed. All the sexually stimulating characteristics were more effective when exaggerated.

In some insects the females search for the males. The ghost

A male ghost swift moth
hovering at twilight over a
grass tuft. Its glistening
white colour reveals it to
searching females.

moth *(Hepialus humuli)* is one of these. In the late dusk at mid-
summer the glistening white males hover over tufts of grass, swinging and gyrating over the same spot for minutes at a time. The
larger dull yellow females fly erratically over the ground, flying up
to males and descending with them to the ground to mate. A white
paper model on a thread has been used successfully to attract the
female, which of course flew away as soon as she had investigated
the dummy.

In several species of dragonfly males have been observed to fly
over streams during the warm part of the day, from about 11.00 to
early evening. Each one guards a territory, driving away trespas-
sers of its own species and others as well. Sometimes they fight and
old males often have tattered wings and amputated legs resulting from these encounters. The females hunt for food over the
countryside at large, occasionally straying over streams. When
this happens the male in occupation of the spot pursues her and
mates with her, if she will accept him, after which she descends
to the water to lay her eggs. The males seem to have little discrimination, and often when flying up to a male trespasser will try to
mate with him first and only attack when the mistake is realized.

The lamplighters

Glow-worms and fireflies (all of which are really beetles) summon
and recognize their prospective mates by means of luminous sig-

nals displayed at night. In the common European glow-worm *(Lampyris noctiluca)* the female is wingless and has the form of a larva. She sits among herbage near the ground and the smaller flying male, whose light is very faint and seems to serve no obvious purpose, uses his well developed eyes to find her.

The North American fireflies have been studied in great detail, and one result of this work has been to show that species that are indistinguishable in preserved museum material can be recognized in the field by the very different combinations of colour and timing of their nocturnal flashes. In many places two or more species of the genus *Photinus* fly together but are prevented from interbreeding, or time-wasting inter-specific approaches, by their distinct light signals. The male of *Photinus pyralis* flies on an undulating course near the ground. At intervals of six seconds he dips down and rises again, giving a half-second flash that appears like a capital 'J' of yellow-green light. If he happens to do this close to a female she responds with a short flash after an interval of two seconds. There are usually two or three repetitions of this performance and then the male descends and mates with her. But she will only respond to capital J's in the air above her at six-second intervals and he will only come down to a flash that follows his signal after two seconds. Another male *Photinus (P. consimilis)* flies two to four metres above the ground and gives out rather slow flashes in groups of three, and a third, *P. granulatus*, flies low emitting quite long flashes during which he jerks rapidly from side to side. At least six patterns have been distinguished.

The sweetsingers

Sclerotin is a substance particularly apt for the formation of stridulating organs, which produce sound by friction in the same way as stroking your finger along the teeth of a comb. They are encountered here and there in several of the insect Orders, but most highly developed for communication in the Orthoptera, the crickets, grasshoppers and their relatives. In the true crickets (Gryllidae) the fore-wings form a cover over the abdomen and a tooth-bearing rib on one of the veins of the right wing is rubbed over a ridge near the hind margin of the left wing. Each wing has both structures developed, but the right one always overlaps the left, and the cricket cannot sing if the positions are reversed; only male crickets produce any sound.

The big shiny black field cricket *(Gryllus campestris)* is now rare in Britain but common in many parts of Europe. It emerges from hibernation in the spring and the males sit at the mouth of their burrows and chirp loudly to attract the females, which are said to respond to them from a distance of up to ten metres. When another cricket approaches his burrow the male produces a more prolonged and vigorous chirp, which is maintained as a challenge if it is another male, and the two will fight unless the trespasser retreats. If the visitor is a female the male produces a third type of song, a quiet ticking sound. This is a courtship song to persuade the female to mate with him.

A male field cricket at the mouth of its burrow.

In the eastern United States study of field crickets has produced the same sort of result as that of fireflies in the same region. At one time it was believed that all the *Gryllus* crickets from Canada down to Florida belonged to one variable species because no structural discontinuities could be found to divide up the thousands of specimens that were examined. Then, in North Carolina, an entomologist found that he could recognize four kinds of field crickets from their songs; they also lived in different habitats and would not hybridize in captivity. Extension of this research over the whole of eastern North America discovered no less than seven species, all of which had previously been 'lumped' as one. They were distinguished, and biologically isolated from each other, by three factors in addition to their distinct songs. Firstly geographical distribution: there are northern and southern species, some distributed with a wide overlap, some quite restricted. They live in different habitats, woodland leaf-litter, rough open ground, relics of prairie or the sea shore. Finally they have different life histories, some maturing in early summer, some later; one of them has two generations in the year. There is overlap in all these factors, but collectively they have had the effect of differentiating the species. Two of the crickets even have songs that are indistinguishable and live in the same area, but as they mature at different times of the year the adults cannot meet. Attempts to hybridize the species have met with varying but always very limited success. When they are divided into species by reference to their biology, differences in size and structure become apparent, but they are not sufficiently marked to be used as separation characters in collections of preserved specimens.

The stridulating apparatus of the bush-crickets or katydids (Tettigoniidae) is similar to that of crickets, but the grasshoppers (Acrididae) produce their music with a different set of instruments. On the inner side of the femur of each hind leg there is a row of minute evenly spaced pegs, which are stroked against the prominent veins of the fore-wings; as in crickets it is the vibration of the wings that produces the sound. It is chiefly the males that sing, but in some species the females also stridulate in reply to the male's serenade. A stridulating grasshopper quite visibly moves its hind legs, rather as a violinist moves his bow, and as in all the vocal insects the species can be readily recognized from their songs. Like the cricket most male grasshoppers have a loud calling song and a more subdued courtship song when the attention of a female has been secured.

Cicadas have the most efficient sound-producing mechanism of any insects and it does not depend on stridulation. It is only present in the males, which have a pair of stiff, ridged membranes called tymbals at the base of the abdomen. These are convex outwards and each has a powerful muscle attached to the concave inner surface. This muscle is of the fibrillar type which supplies power to the wings of bees and flies (p. 24), and its action is to pull the tymbal inwards and then relax, when the tymbal snaps out by its own elasticity. Activated at several hundred times a second this produces the tremendous volume of sound of which many cicadas are capable. The sound is amplified by hollow spaces in the thorax and abdomen, which act as resonators. Much less is known about the mating habits of cicadas than of crickets and grasshoppers. From a study of the North American *Magicicada* (the famous 13-year and 17-year cicadas) it appears that large numbers come to maturity at the same time and when they begin to sing groups of males that happen to be close together act as nuclei or rallying points. Others of both sexes fly to join such a nucleus and as soon as they arrive and settle the males start to call. As more and more cicadas arrive so the noise increases and as the noise increases more join the swarm from greater distances, bringing large numbers of males and females together. It is all rather like a pop festival.

Butterfly courtship

Two examples have been mentioned of a 'courtship' taking place after the meeting of the sexes and before actual mating. In crickets and grasshoppers it has the form of a subdued song, very different from the loud chirping by means of which the female locates the male. In butterflies courtship is easy to observe and has been recorded in a number of cases. After the male and female clouded yellow *(Colias croceus)* meet they fly vertically upwards, circling round each other, and then rapidly descend to the ground to mate. In captivity, in a cage, the male will approach the female, but they do not mate because they are deprived of their preliminary ritual.

Most, probably all, female butterflies have a pheromone by means of which the male confirms his visual identification of his partner, but the males of many species also have a scent which serves a very different purpose. This is carried on certain modified scales on the wings or on tufts of hair on the abdomen. The courtship of the grayling *(Eumenis semele)* has been recorded in detail. The males fly up from the ground to intercept passing females, and if one is ready to mate she will respond by alighting on the ground. The male also alights and takes up a position face to face with her. If she remains motionless he begins his display by jerking his wings upwards and forwards several times and then slowly opening and closing them. At the climax of courtship he opens his fore-wings and then lifts them upwards and forwards in a

The climax in the courtship of a male and female grayling butterfly.

gesture that looks like a deep bow in front of the female. Finally, still in this attitude, he brings his two fore-wings together capturing the female's antennae between them. The male butterfly has a band of scent scales or 'androconia' on each fore-wing and by his final action he delivers the scent to the olfactory organs on the female's antennae. The function of the male's scent is essentially that of an aphrodisiac and plays no part in helping the pair to find each other.

The monarch or milkweed *(Danaus plexippus)* is the only member of the butterfly Family Danaidae ever seen at large in Britain, but in all the warmer parts of the world it is well represented. Among the Danaids the males are equipped with a pair of bundles of hair pencils at the tip of the abdomen, normally concealed but everted during courtship. On the upper surface of each of the male hind-wings there is a pocket into which the hair pencils are inserted when the butterflies are on their own, that is not during courtship. In *Danaus gilippus*, a tropical American species, the male pursues the female and induces her to alight by brushing her antennae with his hair pencils, transferring to them minute particles of scent, and she becomes quiescent and ready to mate. It is supposed that secretions from the hair pencils and the wing glands combine to form the scented substance essential for courtship.

Insect pheromones are seldom perceptible to the human nose, but the scent of male butterflies often is so with a distinctive and sometimes pleasant odour. That of the wall butterfly *(Lasiommata megera)* is sweet like chocolate cream and the male green-veined white *(Pieris napi)* has a strong scent like lemon verbena.

A resting male of the beautiful damselfly *Agrion splendens* reacts to a passing female by bending his abdomen upwards and spreading his wings. The female alights near him and he then performs an aerial fluttering dance around the female before he finally alights on her and assumes the curious posture of dragonfly copulation. Courtship is seen in some other damselflies, but by no means all of them; it has not been observed in dragonflies.

Flies bearing gifts

Some forms of courtship obviously have as their basis the appeasing of a predatory female who might otherwise make a meal of her suitor; it is a conspicuous feature of spider nuptials. Among the insects the dance flies (Empidae) show a series of stages in this sort of behaviour. There are hundreds of species, and in those in which the mating behaviour is regarded as primitive the male simply captures an insect and presents it to the female, who eats it while mating is in progress. Next come species which spin silk from glands on the tarsi of the front legs and wrap their offering in a cocoon. Others, a degree more sophisticated, just proffer a ball of silk, like presenting a lady with an empty chocolate box. In some genera the prey is enclosed in a sphere of froth exuded from the anus, and there are species that offer only a little ball of bubbles onto which is stuck the remains of a victim which the male has already sucked dry; another case of evolutionary progression from a realistic offering to a mere token.

Mating

In mating most of the higher insects couple together, tail to tail, but in the very primitive springtails the male deposits droplets of sperm on the ground, each of which is supported on a stalk. The female takes these up, one by one, into her genital aperture. The droplets are usually deposited at random where numbers of both sexes are present, but in one species that lives on tree trunks the male has been seen to approach and touch a female and then place a ring of sperm droplets all round her so that she cannot avoid encountering them. Another locks his antennae with the female's and pulls or steers her over the droplet which he has produced. This is the common and tiny yellow springtail *Sminthurides aquaticus* which lives on duckweed on the surface of ponds. The equally primitive but unrelated insects called bristletails have a similar indirect mode of insemination, and it can be regarded as one stage removed from that of the aquatic ancestors of insects, which probably released both eggs and sperm into the water.

The majority of male insects introduce their sperm into the female enclosed in a capsule called a spermatophore. In the bush-crickets this is only partially inserted, and it is often eaten by the female while the spermatozoa are entering her body, or it may be removed or fall off. In one genus, *Oecanthus*, the male exudes a secretion from the thorax on which the female feeds while mating. After finishing it she turns and removes the spermatophore, by which time it has discharged its contents. This can be interpreted as an adaptation to divert the female's attention from the sper-matophore until it has fulfilled its purpose. In butterflies and moths

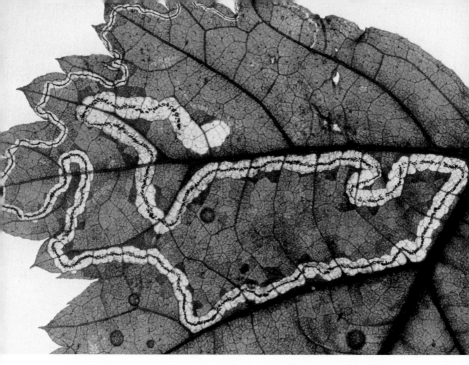

PLATE 5. **Leaf mines.** *Above*, a single mine in a bramble leaf made by the larva of a minute moth, *Nepticula aurella*; *below*, four mines in a leaf of hogweed of the fly *Phytomyza spondylii*. Note how the excrement is disposed in a line in the one and scattered in the other.

PLATE 6. **Modes of feeding.** *Above left*, heart-and-dart moths (*Agrotis exclamationis*) drinking treacle daubed on a fence-post; *right*, breeding and feeding burrows of the ash bark-beetle (*Hylesinus fraxini*), the mating chamber and straight notched egg-channel are below on the right; *below*, larvae of a saw-fly feeding on an aspen leaf.

the spermatophores are passed right into the female's body and retained; in species that mate more than once dissection of a captured female will reveal, by the number of spermatophores in her abdomen, how many husbands she has had.

The males of flies, fleas and some kinds of bugs inject the sperm without any enclosing capsule. The bedbug and its near relatives have a mode of mating which can only be regarded as macabre. The gential organ of the male is a sharp sclerotized hook with which he punctures the abdomen of the female, and his sperm makes its way to her ovaries by way of her blood stream. After mating the wound heals over, and the number of times a female has mated can be ascertained by counting the scars.

The closely related dragonflies and damselflies (Order Odonata) copulate in a curious way which must come to the notice of anyone who spends a little time watching them. The genital opening of the male is in the usual insect position on the underside of the 9th abdominal segment, near the posterior end. But before mating he transfers the sperm to a complicated organ on the underside of his abdomen just behind the thorax. The mode of coupling with the female is not always exactly the same. In the common dragonfly *Sympetrum striolatum* the male approaches the female in flight,

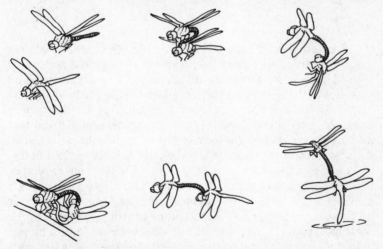

Mating and egg-laying in a dragonfly *Sympetrum striolatum*. The sequence of six stages starts at top *left to right* and continues below, *left to right*. It starts with the male pursuing the female and ends with oviposition with the insects still in tandem.

lands on her back and bends his abdomen round so as to seize her head with a pair of claspers at its tip. He then leaves go with his legs and straightens his abdomen so that his partner is flying below and slightly behind him; the pair are now said to be in tandem. The female then turns upside-down beneath him so as to bring the tip of her abdomen into contact with his accessory genital organ behind his thorax. After transfer of the sperm the two return to the tandem position, and she may lay her eggs with him still attached in this way. Some species of damselflies go under the water in tandem to a depth of 20 cm. or more, crawling down the stems of water plants on which the female lays her eggs.

A female damselfly preparing to lay her eggs while still in tandem with the male.

The external genital organs of insects are sclerotized structures usually regarded as having been derived from paired abdominal appendages. Those of the male often consist of a pair of claspers on each side of the intromittent organ, which are used to hold onto the female. In females a more or less complicated egg-laying organ or ovipositor may be developed. The male external genitalia are often intricately formed and this form is usually highly characteristic of the species, sometimes affording the only reliable method of distinguishing closely similar species from each other. In several of the insect Orders a careful description and drawing of the male genitalia is now an essential adjunct to the description of a species by a taxonomist. This is a general feature of arthropods and may be regarded as a sort of key and lock device to prevent or discourage hybrid matings. It is by no means clear, however, how it works, and visible structures in the female genitalia providing mechanical compatibility with those of the corresponding male are very seldom found.

Reproduction without fertilization of the egg occurs in a variety of insects and is known as parthenogenesis. In many species of stick insects males are either unknown or so rare as to play no significant part in reproduction. Here the egg normally develops without a reduction division of its chromosomes and all the offspring of such eggs are female. Species which reproduce in this way lack the genetic variability which is provided by the interplay of chromosomes and genes in normal sexual reproduction, and it must be supposed that they would be unable to make evolutionary adaptations to changing conditions. Being deprived in this way they must be vulnerable to the sort of hazards that lead to extinction. In many aphids this sort of parthenogenetic reproduction prevails during the summer and leads to very rapid multiplication, but in the autumn individuals of both sexes appear and fertilized eggs are laid, in which form the aphids pass the winter.

Perhaps the strangest type of parthenogenesis is that seen in the honeybee and other bees, wasps and ants. The female or queen stores a large quantity of sperm that she receives from the several drones that mate with her. When she lays an egg she can release at the same time one or a few spermatozoa so that the egg is fertilized; the result is a female, a worker or another queen. She can also withold sperm altogether so that the egg is not fertilized; in this case a male results, and males are produced in no other way. Here the females have the normal diploid or double count of chromosomes, the males being unique among animals in passing normal lives with only the haploid or single number.

INSECT EGGS

Most insects start their active lives by hatching from an egg. There is great diversity in the manner in which the eggs are laid, their numbers and their shape and surface pattern. A few, including stick-insects and some moths simply scatter their eggs on the ground in situations where the emergent larvae are likely to find suitable food; such larvae either feed on a variety of plants or on some ubiquitous sort of grass or herb. More usually the eggs are placed by the female in a situation where the larvae will encounter suitable food immediately on hatching. Most female butterflies and moths seek out plants of the same kind on which they themselves fed as larvae, and stick their eggs to the twigs or leaves. Some species are highly specific in this respect, others feed as larvae on a

variety of plants and their females must depart frequently from the
rule of choosing the food plant on which they themselves subsisted. The holly blue *(Celastrina argiolus)* overwinters in Britain
as a pupa and the spring females usually lay their eggs on the buds
and flowers of holly, and these are the larval food. Butterflies from
this generation fly in the late summer and lay on buds of ivy, inside
which the larvae feed. Here there is clearly no question of individual 'memory' playing any part in the females' choice, and it is
much more likely that the instinct to lay eggs where the larvae will
be correctly nourished is always a matter of inherited behaviour.

Sometimes the deposition of eggs by the female involves quite
complicated behaviour. The bark beetles (Scolytidae) provide an
example of this. They all breed between the bark and the wood in
fallen timber or dying branches of trees, and the beetles and their
larvae excavate burrows half in the wood and half in the bark. Ash
bark beetles *(Hylesinus fraxini)* pair and bore a hole in the bark,
excavating a little oval cell beneath it, the mating chamber. The
female then makes a rather broad, straight egg-channel about 4 cm.
long and cuts an even series of tiny notches along each side of this,
and an egg is laid in each notch. When the larvae hatch they start
burrowing outwards, eating their way through the wood and bark
and growing rapidly. Finally they pupate at the ends of the burrows
and the adult beetles bite their way through the bark to the
exterior. Characteristic patterns are made in bark and wood by
each species, and they are known in America as engraver beetles
(plate 6).

The Odonata, whose nymphs are aquatic, have two distinct
methods of egg laying. The damselflies and the big hawker
dragonflies of the Family Aeshnidae insert their eggs into the stems
and other parts of water plants by making incisions with a serrated
ovipositor. As noted already some damselflies descend below the
surface to do this. This is regarded as the more primitive method.
The more highly evolved dragonflies lay their eggs in flight, sometimes dropping them into the water, more usually flying close to the
surface and making rapid dipping movements in which the tip of
the abdomen is splashed into the water and the eggs washed off.
The female may be alone or flying in tandem with the male.

The number of eggs laid ranges widely, and normally reflects the
sort of hazards to which the larvae are exposed. These are usually
severe and 100 to several hundred eggs is a normal quantity. The
female oil beetle *(Meloe)* lays a number of batches of eggs on the

A selection of butterflies' eggs to show diversity in form and ornamentation. *Left to right*, large white, white admiral, gatekeeper, small copper, brown argus, red admiral.

ground, the total number amounting to several thousand. The tiny active larvae swarm over plants and seize onto any hairy insect that happens to come near enough, and the insect flies away with the beetle larva attached. Probably only a small minority encounter an insect at all, but of those that do so only the ones that happen to have caught hold of a particular kind of solitary bee will survive, as they can only feed on the eggs and stored honey and pollen in the nests of the bees; they are in fact a nest parasite of the bee. With such an exceedingly hazardous start to their lives there is no wonder that huge numbers of eggs are needed to maintain the continued existence of oil beetles.

The eggs of insects usually hatch soon after they are laid, or they may lie dormant over the winter or over a dry season. Stick insects are curiously irregular in their reproductive habits. Not only are many of them parthenogenetic, but in some species the hard seed-like eggs are known to lie on the ground for nearly two years.

Insects' eggs show great diversity in shape and pattern, especially those which are laid in situations exposed to the elements and so require protective adaptations. Those of butterflies are laid in the open and have a hard impermeable shell. This may be smooth or sculptured, and the shape and appearance of the eggs is usually characteristic of the butterfly Family concerned. The swallowtails lay smooth round eggs; those of the Pieridae are bottle-shaped and finely ridged. The Nymphalid butterflies usually have eggs with few and prominent ribs.

Strictly speaking all insects develop from eggs, but sometimes these hatch in the body of the female, so that the insect is effectively viviparous. This is true of the parthenogenetic generations of aphids which multiply so rapidly in summer. An aphid can give birth to a dozen or so young in the course of twenty-four hours, and when they are abundant only a strong lens and a moderate amount of patience is needed if one wishes to witness aphid births. A more

Reproduction in the tsetse fly. The female gives birth to a single, fully-developed larva (*left*); this (*top right*) burrows into the ground and turns into a brown puparium.

genuine sort of viviparity is found among certain blood-sucking flies. Most of these are external parasites of mammals and birds, the sheep ked, *Melophagus ovinus*, being a typical example. This is a wingless spider-like insect that passes its life in the fleece of sheep. The larva hatches in the uterus of the female and is nourished with liquid from glands in the mother's body which open near its mouth. It grows to full size before it is born and pupates immediately after leaving its mother's body. The notorious tsetse fly of tropical Africa is quite unrelated to the Pupipara, the group that includes the sheep ked, but has developed a similar type of reproduction. This is presumably because it is also a blood-sucker and so able to nourish its offspring internally until its growth is completed. Reproduction of this sort is in direct contrast with that of the oil beetle; the young is completely protected by the active and wary mother fly, and in the course of her life of six months the tsetse fly produces no more than twelve offspring, a far lower potential than that of a rabbit.

GROWTH AND METAMORPHOSIS

The stages by which insects come to maturity after leaving the egg show a gradation from simple growth in the primitive wingless insects to the profound changes of form or metamorphosis seen in highly evolved insects like butterflies. Growth always proceeds discontinuously, as in all arthropods, interrupted by moulting of the cuticle. The very great differences between the way in which insects and humans grow up calls for the use of a number of special terms in entomology, which it will be well to define here for easy reference; Latin plurals and adjectival forms are put in brackets.

Metamorphosis (metamorphoses). The sum total of the changes undergone by an insect in the course of its growth.
Ecdysis (ecdyses). The act of moulting or shedding the cuticle.
Stadium (stadia). The interval or stage between two ecdyses.

Instar. The form assumed by an insect during any particular stadium, as *pupal instar.*

Larva (larvae, larval). The caterpillar or grub which precedes the pupa of an insect with complete metamorphosis. The larval form persists through several stadia during which the whole of the insect's growth is completed.

Nymph. Term often used in preference to larva for the pre-adult stages of insects which have incomplete metamorphosis. The nymph persists for a number of stadia and develops into an adult without any pupal instar.

Pupa (pupae, pupal). The usually inert resting instar between the last larval stadium and the imago. Some insects, e.g. mosquitoes, have active pupae. 'Chrysalis' is a term, whose use has declined, for the pupa of butterflies.

Imago (imagines, imaginal). The adult or final instar of an insect that undergoes metamorphosis.

The presence or absence of the wings and the way they develop during metamorphosis forms the basis on which insects are classified. Three main groups are recognized. In the most primitive *(Apterygota)* the wings are absent and we can be sure from various lines of evidence that these insects have been wingless throughout their evolutionary history. In them the young closely resemble the adults in all respects except size, so there is no metamorphosis. In the next grade, the *Exopterygota*, the wings develop outside the body, appearing first as little pads which become larger in each successive instar. The young or nymphs of exopterygote insects generally resemble the adults fairly closely, differing chiefly in the absence of functional wings, so their metamorphosis is incomplete. The most highly developed insects are the *Endopterygota* in which the wing rudiments grow inwards until the next-to-last instar, the pupa, when they appear clearly outside the body. The very profound changes from larva to pupa and pupa to imago constitute complete metamorphosis. The three names mean, by derivation, 'not-winged', 'outward-winged' and 'inward-winged'. There are many wingless insects among the Exopterygota and Endopterygota, but all of these betray in one way or another the fact that they are descended from winged evolutionary ancestors.

No better example of the Apterygota could be selected than the little silverfish *(Lepisma saccharina)* of our kitchen cupboards. This is a remarkable insect in more ways than one. It seems now to be a purely domestic species, not known anywhere in an outdoor habitat. In a Chinese dictionary compiled between the 4th and 2nd centuries BC it is recognizably described, and was already a dweller in houses. At the same time it is a 'living fossil', a survivor of the sort of insects that evolved from centipede-like ancestors between 400 and 300 million years ago, and it possesses the structures called paranota from which the wings of insects are believed to be derived, but in the silverfish's long family history they remained paranota (p. 20). The female lays eggs from which tiny individuals hatch, differing from their parents only in size and having the same habit of creeping about at night and scavenging on any sort of crumbs and smears derived from human foodstuffs. As they grow they repeatedly shed their skins and on reaching a certain size start breeding, but continue ecdysis and growth after this. A silverfish may moult fifty or more times during its surprisingly long life of several years.

A grasshopper is a typical exopterygote insect. The hatchling is recognizably a grasshopper, but it has no wings. In the course of growing up it moults 5 to 8 times, and after the first or second ecdysis the wings appear as little pads on each side of the thorax. With each successive moult these are bigger until finally they are completely developed and the insect can fly. At this stage it also becomes sexually mature, and it never moults again. Bugs (Hemiptera) have a similar sort of life history. Almost all insects cease to moult when their wings are fully formed. The mayflies (Ephemeroptera) are the one exception; they moult once again after emerging from the water and developing their wings.

The metamorphosis of the endopterygote insects is another thing altogether. A grasshopper nymph is a young grasshopper, but a caterpillar is not a young butterfly. It is more realistic to regard it as a worm-like animal that lives its life of eating and growing and periodical ecdysis and then, when it pupates, ends this life and is reincarnated as a butterfly. When a caterpillar hangs itself up to pupate, or spins its silken cocoon, a process called histolysis commences whereby almost all of its muscles, and those of its internal organs that cannot serve the imago, are destroyed by wandering blood cells called phagocytes, which digest and liquify them. The substance so produced provides the material and energy for building up the organs and appendages of the imago. These arise for the most part from clumps of cells called imaginal buds, which have resisted the process of dissolution and remained alive. In this way the substance of the larva is reconstituted to form a butterfly. The wings, arising from inwardly growing imaginal buds, are everted, and these, and the new legs, antennae and mouth-parts, are formed at pupation and can be seen in outline on the shell of the pupa. Formation of the adult internal organs continues after pupation. Histolysis and regeneration occurs in varying degrees, and there is relatively little in the more primitive Endopterygota such as the lacewings and alder-flies, some of whose larval organs pass over with little alteration to serve the adult insect.

Larvae show a great range of structural variation and are adapted to a wide range of environments. They can be classified into three main types in order of decreasing activity. The first is the *campodeiform* larva, so called because it has the general appearance and structure of a primitive apterygote insect, such as the silverfish, but another genus, *Campodea*, has been chosen to provide a name for this larval type. These larvae have the three pairs of thoracic legs well developed and the head and thorax are sclerotized. As in *Campodea* and other apterygotes there is a pair of cerci at the tail end. The lacewings and their allies have larvae of this type and so do some kinds of beetles. Next are the *eruciform* larvae (*eruca* is the Latin for a caterpillar) of the Lepidoptera, sawflies and scorpion-flies or Mecoptera. The head is sclerotized, but not the thorax, and there are usually unsegmented abdominal feet, often called claspers or prolegs. The larvae of some beetles are also classified as eruciform; among them are the ladybirds. Larvae that live surrounded by their food, or are fed by 'nurses' of their own species, are usually legless and constitute the third type, the *apodous* larva, to which the term 'maggot' is equally applicable. Flies, ants, bees and wasps, and some kinds of beetles have apodous larvae.

To some extent this classification represents a progress from a primitive type to specialized types of various kinds, but the fact that all three forms are found among one Order, the beetles, and that both the very primitive scorpion-flies and the highly evolved Lepidoptera have eruciform larvae shows that it does not reflect the basic classification of insects. Larval form is much more a matter of adaptation to a more or less active mode of life, and to various modes of feeding, than of evolutionary origin.

THE PUPA STAGE

Pupae are primarily classified according to whether they have functional mandibles. These are present in some primitive Orders, the lacewings, scorpion-flies, caddisflies and a few tiny moths

which have been excluded by some authorities from the Lepidoptera and put in an Order of their own. The mandibles are used for
breaking out of the cocoon or pupal cell at ecdysis. The pupae are
called *decticous* and represent an evolutionary stage earlier than
any of the jawless or *adecticous* pupae of the higher endopterygote
insects. Among these a further subdivision is made; it is very
unequal, but the smaller division is the more familiar one, due to
the frequent practice of breeding butterflies and moths in captivity.
Their pupae are variously formed but are uniform in having an
intact surface in which the wings, legs and antennae are visible but
appear to be stuck down or embedded. This is the *obtect* pupa. In
the far more general *exarate* pupa of almost all other insects that
pupate the wings, legs and antennae are free and loosely folded
against the body. The appendages are without any effective power
of movement and are in fact enclosed in closely fitting sheaths from
which they will be withdrawn at ecdysis. Many exarate pupae are
white or pale coloured and look like bedraggled and apparently
lifeless adults. Among the beetles the ladybirds (which have an
eruciform larva) are also peculiar in having an obtect pupa, a
condition obviously associated with their habit of pupating in the
open, stuck down on leaves or stems.

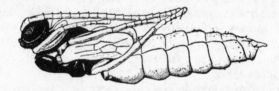

A typical exarate pupa. (From A. D. Imms *Insect Natural History*, Collins.)

Pupae are often enclosed in a cell in the earth or excavated in soft
wood, or they may be protected by a cocoon which the larva makes
of silk spun from glands which open just below its mouth. The
cocoon of a moth is of course the foundation of the silk industry.
The more advanced flies, including house-flies and bluebottles,
appear superficially to have a pupa of a type peculiar to themselves. When their maggot-larvae pupate the result is a brown or
blackish ovate structure, smooth and without any trace of appendages or segments on its surface. This, however, is not the
pupa but a kind of cocoon formed of the last larval skin at the
time of pupation. It contains a normal exarate pupa.

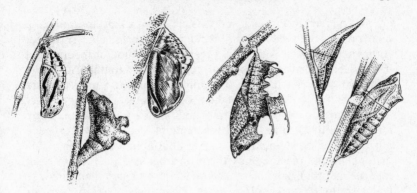

Examples to show diversity in butterfly pupae. *Left to right*, meadow brown, *Jacoona jusana*, *Euploea midamus*, *Vindula arsinoe*, orange-tip, common swallowtail. The three not named in English are Malaysian species.

Reverting to the pupae of butterflies and moths it is interesting to note that although the moths are far more numerous and diverse than the butterflies, butterfly pupae show much greater diversity than moth pupae. The great majority of the latter are variously sized brown or black bullet-like objects which even the most sophisticated lepidopterists can seldom identify with confidence. Butterfly pupae are variously and specifically shaped and coloured, many having spines or other outgrowths from the cuticle; they are often effectively camouflaged in the surroundings in which the larva normally pupates. The explanation is of course that in almost all moths the pupa is concealed in a cocoon, and this in turn is hidden, often underground. In these natural selection does nothing to promote elaboration in the appearance of the pupa as this would serve no protective purpose. Butterfly pupae are almost always exposed and so gain advantage from any appearance that will conceal them from predators or (in some cases) advertise the fact that they are inedible. In the case of the far more numerous camouflaged pupae their very diversity protects them; if they conformed to a single pattern, even one giving effective concealment, their enemies would have only one image to keep in mind when searching for them.

FEEDING

The feeding of insects falls conveniently into four modes. There are those that bite and chew solid food and those that take up only liquids and feed by piercing and sucking or by licking and sponging them up, and both these groups include herbivores and carnivores. Biting and chewing is the less specialized method of feeding and insects that subsist in this way tend to have mouthparts of the primitive 'cockroach' type. The foliage of plants supports more insects than any other class of diet, so let us look at a hungry locust as it comes down from the sky and settles on some unhappy farmer's field of maize. Its strong mandibles cut piece after piece out of a leaf or stem, the maxillae and labium and their palps manipulate the pieces, pack them together and push them back into the mouth. Caterpillars feed on leaves in much the same way and with similar oral equipment. Provided it is not at large in your garden, it is a pleasure to watch a caterpillar slowly reducing the area of a leaf by precise repetitive snipping at its edge. The Lepidoptera are surely the most attractive group of insects, and one feature that makes them so is the tidy and interesting table manners of their larvae. Many of the leaf beetles (Chrysomelidae) feed as larvae and adults on leaves, usually specializing in one or several closely allied kinds of plants. The notorious Colorado beetle is one of these.

Plant cells have walls of cellulose which must be broken to release their fluid contents, since these are the real source of nourishment for almost all herbivorous animals. Mammals like cattle, horses and grass-eating rodents need to grind their meals up with special mill-like molar teeth, but the small mandibles of insects bite so precisely and minutely that most of the cells are ruptured in the act of feeding and further mastication is unnecessary.

A very special mode of feeding on leaves is that of the leaf-miners, most of which are the larvae of small moths or flies. The minute eggs are laid singly on leaves and the larva bites its way into the leaf and then eats out a space between the upper and lower epidermis, feeding on the palisade and parenchyma cells. Some miners make a winding linear burrow that widens as the larva grows, so that it looks curiously like a river as depicted on a map; as the larva progresses it leaves behind it a trail of minute excremental pellets. Other species mine outwards from a centre and make a 'blotch mine', or a linear one may widen into a blotch at its later end. On reaching maturity some of the larvae pupate in the mine, other species leave the leaf and descend to the ground. A surprising number of leaf-miners is found in the British fauna, over 100 tiny moths in the Families Nepticulidae and Gracillariidae and an even larger total among flies of various Families, particularly the Agromyzidae. Entomologists who study these insects have found that the form of the mine and the way in which the excrement is disposed in it, together of course with the species of plant involved, is of value in identifying the insect species. Some of them are more readily determined by this means than by examination of the imago.

Feeding inside the stems of herbs is a habit of many insect larvae, ranging over various insect Orders. The wainscot moths of the genera *Archanara* and *Nonagria* are internal feeders in rushes and reeds during their larval stadia, and the larvae and pupae can be found by seeking reeds in which the top central shoot is yellow or withered and splitting open the stem lower down. Some species invariably pupate head-upward in the stem, others head-downward. A small moth of the Family Pyralidae, known in America as the European corn-borer, feeds in the same way in the stems of maize and is a serious pest. It is indeed a southern European species, *Pyrausta nubilalis*, one of many unfortunate trans-Atlantic introductions into America, and it occurs as a rarity in Britain. It feeds in the stems of various plants, but maize is of course an adopted food plant since it is endemic to the New World.

Eaters of wood

No vegetable substance escapes the appetite of insects, and many larvae feed on wood, living or dead. The majority are those of beetles, and I have already referred to the bark or engraver beetles whose small larvae tunnel between bark and wood. One large Family of beetles, the longicorns or longhorns (Cerambycidae) burrow deeply in wood, living and dead, and some are serious enemies of forestry. Some of the beautiful jewel beetles (Buprestidae) also have harmful wood-boring larvae. The food value of wood is low and larvae living in it often take a long time to come to maturity. One North American beetle, living in the heartwood of yellow pine, has been observed to live as a larva for over 40 years. The house longhorn beetle *(Hylotrupes bajulus)* feeds as a larva in softwood structural timber in Europe and the life cycle is usually between 3 and 6 years, but as long as 32 years has been recorded.

Other notorious wood borers are the furniture beetle *(Anobium punctatum)* and the death watch beetle *(Xestobium rufovillosum)*. Both these bore as larvae in dead wood, and the furniture beetle is found in wooden furniture, wicker work and the timber of houses. Its presence can be recognized by the exit holes on the surface of the wood, which are a little over 1 mm. in diameter. Known commonly as 'woodworm' it is a serious pest in houses, whose timber may be reduced to a honeycomb condition resulting in structural collapse. A recent survey has revealed that three-quarters of the houses in Britain harbour *Anobium*. The death watch beetle is more of a menace to old houses and churches and cathedrals due to its preference for old oak, and to the fact that it does not fly readily and so seldom invades buildings anew. It is thought that infestation is usually the result of using wood that already harbours the larvae. Both *Anobium* and the death watch are commonly found in dead wood out of doors, and in the days before demand so greatly exceeded supply, timber was often left in the open to 'season' for periods long enough to incur the risk of infection. The death watch is the larger species, its exit holes in the wood being about 3 mm. in diameter.

Other borers and feeders in live wood include the larvae of the goat and leopard moths (Family Cossidae) and of the wood wasps (Siricidae) which are allied to saw-flies. Some of these are destructive in pine plantations. Goat moth caterpillars take three years to reach full size in the wild, but it is said that if the young larvae are fed on beetroot they will mature in a year. Termites form an Order of wood-eating insects on their own, and their habits will be described when we come to the social insects.

After the eaters of the living and solid substance of plants we will turn to the detritus and saprophagous feeders. As they include much of the teeming soil populations they must rival the plant feeders in numbers if not in biomass; the soil insects are mostly very small. The distinction implied by the two terms is that saprophages eat substances transformed by decay and detritus feeders subsist on the original animal and vegetable proteins, but it is complicated by the fact that many saprophages feed mainly on the fungi that promote decay, and it is difficult to maintain because detritus passes gradually into mould and humus. I shall use just detritus feeding as a convenient simplification.

Most of the tiny springtails and bristletails come into this class, and among larger insects the cockroaches subsist in the wild state by detritus feeding and scavenging. It is of interest to note that this type of feeding, combined with preference for a rather dry climate, seems to be the background of most of the 'domestic' insects, the silverfish and firebrat and the several species of cockroaches that have invaded our houses. Relatives of the two domestic bristle-tails are rather common under stones in dry and warm-temperate climates, and the commonest domestic cockroaches are believed to be natives of northern Africa.

A curious and special type of detritus feeding has been reported from the very dry Namib desert of south-western Africa. Winds blowing from the interior of the continent carry dust consisting largely of dry, finely divided vegetable matter. This settles in drifts in the hollows of the dunes and provides food for the Tenebrionid beetles that are almost the only insects found there.

Feeders on dung

Animal dung is a particular form of detritus often quite rich in nutrients due to incomplete digestion of vegetable food. A variety of insects have specialized in feeding on it including the larvae of various flies, but the most important and interesting are the dung beetles of the superfamily Scarabaeoidea. The common British dor beetle *Geotrupes stercorarius* pays particular attention to cow-pats, and the male and female work in partnership: a tunnel 40 to 60 cm. deep is excavated beneath the deposit, this being mainly the work of the female, who goes on to dig out brood chambers at its base or laterally from the main shaft. The male then sets to work on the dung, taking it down to the female, who kneads it into sausage-shaped masses which are pushed into the brood chambers, each of which then receives a single egg; each chamber is provided with enough food for the development of one larva. While engaged on this strenuous work the beetles fortify themselves with dung, and throughout the country huge quantities are taken underground, to the great benefit of the pasture land.

The great French naturalist Henri Fabre studied the habits of another species, *Onthophagus taurus*. Here the male, who has a pair of slender horns on his head, gives the female no help in digging or stocking food for their offspring. She alone bores a shaft beneath sheep dung, excavates a chamber at its base and puts in a mass of dung and a single egg, sealing the chamber with dung when she has finished.

The most celebrated of the coprophagous beetles is the sacred beetle of ancient Egypt, *Scarabaeus sacer*. This is one of the species which make balls of dung and roll them from their source to

Two scarab beetles rolling a ball of dung in search of a place to bury it.

a place suitable for burrowing, that is with loose soil and preferably in the shade. The sacred scarab is a beetle about 4 cm. long, strong and compact, as it needs to be since its dung-balls are sometimes as big as a man's fist. In most cases a large burrow is dug into which the beetle, of either sex, pushes the ball and then feeds on it, emerging later to seek more food. When dung is collected for the larvae the female does all the work, burying the ball in a large brood chamber a few inches deep. After the egg is laid in an open cavity hollowed in the ball the outside of the ball is smoothed and plastered down and moulded to a pear shape with a tough rind which protects the food store and the larva from drying up. Often two beetles are found rolling a ball in what looks like partnership, but it is always made by a single individual and the one that joins in the rolling may do so with an unworthy motive. If the attention of the rightful owner is distracted the other beetle is likely to trundle it rapidly away and appropriate it for its own use. The largest ball rollers are the African and Indian species of *Heliocopris*, which deal efficiently with huge piles of elephant dung. The food stores that they make for their larvae are coated with clay and have been mistaken for old cannon balls.

 In the limestone caves of Malaya and Borneo huge populations of bats and the small birds called swiftlets roost and nest in the roofs and their droppings accumulate on the floor. These consist mostly of indigestible parts of insects, especially the hard parts of flying beetles, and as this 'guano' decomposes it provides food for vast numbers of insects. The most conspicuous of these are cockroaches of the genus *Pycnoscelis* which often cover the surface, 3,000 or more to the square metre. Another very obvious guanophage is the small moth *Tinea palaeochrysis*, hundreds of which fly continuously like little ghosts just above the surface. It is as larvae that they eat the guano, and each little caterpillar lives in a

PLATE 7. Oak beauty moth (*Biston strataria*) at rest on an oak trunk.

PLATE 8. **Industrial melanism.** A spotted and a black peppered moth (*Biston betularia*) are shown resting on a lichened oak trunk (*above*) and on a soot-blackened pine trunk.

case like that of a caddis worm, which it drags around as it crawls in search of food.

The swiftlets make bracket-like nests of matted and hardened strings of their own viscous saliva, and these are the valuable birds' nests so greatly relished by the Chinese. The larva of a small moth, *Pyralis pictalis*, has anticipated the appetite of the Chinese for coagulated mucus and lives in and on the nests, riddling them and often causing them to fall before the young birds are fledged.

Another peculiar example of scavenging below the living quarters of other animals is that of the larvae of *Volucella*, a genus of large hover-flies, which live in the bottom of wasps' and bees' nests, underneath the combs. This is the depository for all inhabitants of the nest who die at home and for the mass of faecal matter cleaned out of the cells by the workers after the pupae have hatched, and the fly larvae subsist on this accumulation. These hover-flies breed only in this situation and the females enter the nests to lay their eggs unharmed by its formidable residents.

When a large animal dies in the open the first insects to pay attention to it are blow-flies and flesh-flies, which quickly come and lay their eggs. The maggots that hatch can absorb only liquid food. This is provided by the action of their own excretions, which break down and liquify the decomposing tissues and also by the lacerating action of their 'mouth-hooks', which are not true jaws, though they are used as such.

As the carcase dries these pupate and complete their life history, and various beetles and their larvae use the remaining skin and ligament as food. In the final stages of desiccation and decay the Dermestid beetles take over. This is the Family that includes the larder, carpet and fur beetles which invade houses and attack stored food and any substance of animal origin such as furs and wool. The fur beetle (*Attagenus pellio*) is often a pest of insect collections. The very young larvae make their way through chinks in cabinet drawers and store-boxes, and the collection is soon reduced to rows of pins with heaps of dust around them. On the other hand Dermestid beetles sometimes serve a useful purpose in museums. When skeletons of large animals are being prepared as specimens it is difficult to remove all traces of decomposable matter and so prevent the bones from creating a smelly nuisance that may endure for years. If they are put well apart from the collections and a culture of suitable beetles is introduced, these and their larvae will feed and breed until even a Dermestid can find nothing more to feed on.

Predatory insects

Turning now to the predators, there are good reasons for awarding the first place among them to the dragonflies. These are the falcons of the insect world, highly specialized for hunting other insects on the wing. With their huge and efficient eyes they can spot a victim ten metres away. Of the insects whose speed of flight has been measured the swiftest is a large dragonfly. The structure of the thorax is modified so that the lower part of it, which carries the legs, is displaced forwards. The result of this is that the six spiny legs, when outstretched, form a forwardly directed net or basket in which the prey is captured in mid-air. This has involved a sacrifice of the legs as a means of locomotion; dragonflies are seldom seen to walk and do so quite inefficiently. When one of them catches a large victim it usually alights to eat it, and the snapping and crunching of its jaws can be heard several feet away. The delicate damselflies (which are often included under the term 'dragonfly') are no less ferocious but of course prey on much smaller insects and sometimes pick them off vegetation instead of catching them in flight.

The head of a dragonfly nymph showing the mask at rest (*left*) and in use to catch a worm. (From M. C. Chinery *A Field Guide to the Insects of Britain and Northern Europe*, Collins.)

The nymphs of dragonflies are also fierce predators of aquatic insects, tadpoles and small fish. In them the labium is hinged on its joints and folded back under the head, and its palps have taken the form of sharp claws. When it sees anything small and moving the nymph approaches stealthily to about a centimetre and then the labium (often called the mask) shoots out, the claws grasp the victim and it is drawn back to the mouth. The segments of the mask are extended by pumping body fluid into them, not by muscular action.

Most of the beetles of the Family Carabidae are carnivorous and some are quick active hunters with long legs and large, sharply pointed jaws. Tiger beetles (Cicindelidae) are so equipped and also

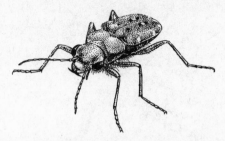

A tiger beetle; the long, sharp jaws show it to be a predator.

have large eyes, and they hunt other insects by sight in open sandy places on heaths. Although they fly readily all their hunting is done on the ground where they can run at a speed of 60 cm. a second, or 1½ miles per hour. This may not seem very fast, but tiger beetles are small animals. In order to cover its own length as speedily as a tiger beetle does a racehorse 8 feet long would have to run at about 250 m.p.h. Other kinds of Carabids dig for burrowing insects and moth pupae, and there are species which climb trees and hunt for caterpillars, bush-crickets and the like. One of these is the beautiful European *Calosoma sycophanta,* which was deliberately introduced to North America to prey on the larvae of the accidentally introduced gypsy moth. The beetle is now well established in the regions where the moth is present and is said to be doing good service in controlling the pest, though it must destroy large numbers of harmless caterpillars as well.

Ladybirds (Coccinellidae) and their larvae are also predatory. They are slow moving because their normal prey is aphids, which are even slower, and scale-insects which do not move at all. Far more than Carabids the ladybirds are friends of the farmer and gardener as aphids and scale insects are extremely harmful: several kinds of ladybirds have been used as agents in biological control.

Praying mantises or mantids are predators of a rather different kind because they do not pursue their prey but lie in ambush for it. The fore-legs have the tibia and femur opposed to each other like the blade and handle of a penknife, and both are armed with spines which interlock when the apparatus is closed. Insects, and sometimes small lizards or birds, which unwittingly approach the mantis, are seized with a lightning-quick grab of the spined legs and then held to the mouth and eaten alive with small delicate bites, like a lady eating a sandwich. Most of the mantids are tropical or

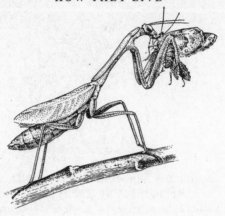

The praying mantis lies in wait for its prey and seizes it with its fore-legs; this one is eating a butterfly.

subtropical and all of them are camouflaged, either green or brown to simulate live or dead foliage, or more elaborately to resemble flowers. In all cases the camouflage serves the double purpose of deceiving the prey and protecting the mantis from its enemies such as birds and large lizards.

Feeding by suction

I could describe many more kinds of biting insects, but it is time to turn away from them to the ones that take only liquid food. Most of these have some kind of proboscis which pierces the tissues of plants or animals or probes flowers for their nectar.

This section began with an Order of insects, the Odonata, which without exception are predators that chew up their prey with their jaws. The bugs or Hemiptera do not feed within quite such a narrow spectrum, but they all have piercing and sucking mouth-parts and take liquid food, which may be vegetable or animal. The greater number of them, comprising a very large total, feed on the sap of plants, many prey on other insects and some suck the blood of vertebrate animals. In considering their complicated feeding apparatus we encounter the interesting principle that almost all the elements of the mouth-parts of the various sucking insects can be derived, by reference to their development and arrangement, from the primitive 'tool-kit' of labium and labrum, mandibles and maxillae, seen in cockroaches and beetles.

In the bugs a rostrum or beak can be seen, folded back under the head and thorax when not in use, extended downwards at a right angle to the body when the bug is feeding. The rostrum comprises an outer sheath, the labium, containing two pairs of extremely fine and slender stylets, which are highly modified mandibles and maxillae. The labial sheath is not a closed sleeve but is open along its front surface; when the rostrum is applied to the surface of the food source the sheath buckles or 'elbows' backwards leaving the stylets exposed above their point of penetration. They never separate but operate as a tight, slender bundle with the mandibles outside and the maxillae inside and interlocking to form two very slender tubes, an anterior suction tube and a posterior salivary tube. In some bugs the mandibles can move independently, sliding past each other, and they may be backwardly barbed. Moving alternately each one acts as an anchor while the other probes deeper. As the insect feeds it injects saliva which usually has the effect of partly digesting the food and so making it more fluid. This is particularly the case in the blood feeders, such as the bed-bug, as the blood must be prevented from clotting and so blocking the narrow suction tube. In many of the predatory bugs the saliva is also poisonous and serves to paralyse and kill the victim.

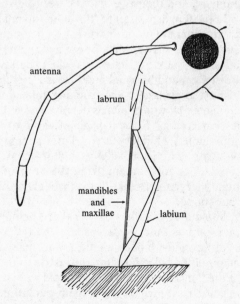

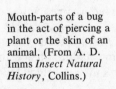

Mouth-parts of a bug in the act of piercing a plant or the skin of an animal. (From A. D. Imms *Insect Natural History*, Collins.)

antenna

labrum

mandibles and maxillae

labium

A winged and wingless aphid of the same species. All aphids feed by sucking the sap
of plants.

The bugs are divided into two very distinct suborders, the
Homoptera and Heteroptera. The former include aphids and
cicadas and are all feeders on sap, a food containing much sugar
and little protein. Excess sugar is excreted as a clear sweet solution, and this is the 'honeydew' produced in great quantities by
aphids and much relished by ants. Cicadas produce it in quite large
drops and one may get the impression that it is raining under a tree
where numbers of them are feeding among the branches. The other
group of bugs, the Heteroptera, are also mostly plant feeders, but
quite a number are predators. Among these are the assassin bugs
(Reduviidae) which attack both other insects and vertebrate
animals, and their bite may be very poisonous and painful.

In the female mosquito (the males do not feed on blood) a similar
arrangement of mouth-parts is found: a bundle of slender stylets is
enclosed in a labial sheath, open along its front margin; as in the
bugs this buckles backwards when the stylets pierce one's skin.
Both the mandibles and maxillae are piercing organs, the maxillae
being the stronger. The sucking tube is formed by the greatly
elongated labrum, which is deeply grooved, like the labium, so that
it forms a canal. Since it originates above the mouth the opening or
slit is along its hinder margin. This opening is closed by yet another
elongate extension of the mouth-parts, the hypopharynx, a
tongue-like lobe arising from the floor of the mouth. Inside the
hypopharynx is a closed tube through which saliva is pumped into
the wound.

Mosquitoes are flies (Diptera) and belong to the Endopterygota;
bugs are exopterygote insects, and the two groups certainly
evolved quite independently. The manner in which they have
adapted the basic insect mouth-parts to the same end, making use
of them in a similar but not identical way, provides a good example
of what is known as convergent evolution.

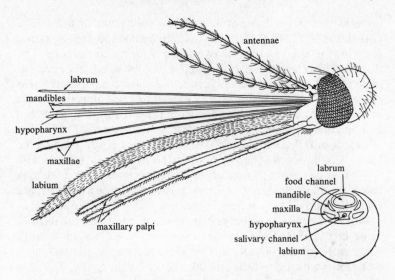

Diagram of the side of the head and mouth-parts of a female mosquito, the stylets being separated from the groove of the labium. On the right is a transverse section showing the position of the stylets in the grooves of the labium. (From A. D. Imms *Insect Natural History*, Collins.)

Some insect larvae have piercing and sucking mouth-parts of relatively simple design. The fierce predatory larvae of the big *Dytiscus* water beetles have long curved mandibles, pointed at the tip and grooved so deeply that they are in effect tubular. The channel is open at the base and at the tip, and a digestive fluid is pumped into the prey, quickly killing it, and its tissues are dissolved and sucked back into the pharynx.

Insects which suck up exposed liquids, such as honeydew or the nectar of flowers, also have a tube formed from some feature of the mouth-parts, but no mechanism for piercing is needed. In the honeybee the end of the labium is extended to form a flexible tongue or glossa, which is grooved in the usual way, so deeply that it forms an almost closed tube. It is surrounded and protected by the elongated maxillae above and the labial palps below. The mandibles are normally developed but are small and blunt and are used for moulding the wax of which the comb is formed.

The coiled tongue of butterflies and moths is a remarkable structure. It is formed from the maxillary lobes called galeae which are greatly elongated and grooved along their inner surfaces. The two galeae are held together by minute hooks and spines, rather like a zip fastener, so that the two grooves form a closed tube. The way in which the proboscis is coiled and uncoiled has been explained in more than one way; it seems most probable that it is extended by forcing blood into a channel that lies along the inside of each galea. When the blood is withdrawn it coils up again by a combination of its own elastic tendency to do so and of the action of minute muscles which lie in the channels that are invaded by the blood. In some of the big hawkmoths which feed from flowers with a long corolla tube the length of the proboscis is remarkable. It may reach 25 cm. in the largest tropical hawkmoths, considerably more than the span of their wings.

Most butterflies feed on nectar or the juice of fallen fruit, but some of the Heliconiidae of the New World eat pollen as well. They gather it in sticky lumps on their probosces, moistening it with saliva which dissolves and digests the pollen grains. The fluid so obtained is sucked up and nourishes the insect. This consumption of a protein diet is associated with the very long life of the Heliconiid butterflies, which may fly actively for six months.

There is a group of tropical moths allied to the European and North American red and crimson underwings (Catocalinae), whose proboscis is stiffened and adapted for piercing the rind of fruit so that the moth can feed on the juice. One of these, *Othreis fullonia*, is a pest in the northern Australian citrus orchards. The fruit attacked by it does not appear to suffer much injury, but it is always infected with fungus spores and quickly decays. Even more extraordinary is the Malayan species *Calpe eustrigata* that uses its proboscis to pierce the skin of large mammals such as buffaloes and feed on their blood. Its discoverer, Dr H. Bänziger, had no difficulty in persuading a specimen to feed from his hand and arm.

The flies of the house-fly and bluebottle type are regarded as the most highly evolved flies and they take liquid food by 'mopping it up' and then sucking it along a tube. In them the feeding organ is the labium, which has a stem, grooved to form the feeding channel, and a pair of expanded lobes at the tip. The lobes are called labella and have numerous branching grooves and tubes which converge on the end of the channel. They are called pseudotracheae because they have a structure similar to the true tracheae of the breathing system. When the labella are pressed against a wet surface the pseudotracheae take up the liquid by capillary action and lead it to

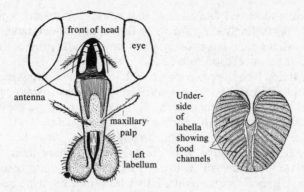

Head of house-fly, seen from the front, and under-side of labella or 'tongue' (highly magnified). (From A. D. Imms *Insect Natural History*, Collins.)

the feeding tube. Close inspection of a feeding fly will show just how the apparatus is operated.

In some of the higher flies the labella have developed what appears to be a secondary modification to enable the insects to feed on blood. Both the stable-fly *(Stomoxys)* and the notorious tsetse-fly have minute teeth on the tips of the labella with which they cut through the skin of animals, including man, and mop up the blood which exudes. The stable-fly looks very much like a house-fly but its bite is quite painful and is usually marked by a spot of blood if the fly is swatted or frightened away. With this brief survey we must leave the subject of insect feeding for yet another aspect of their way of life.

PROTECTION AGAINST PREDATORS

Needless to say the innumerable insects have innumerable enemies. Those that take the greatest toll of them are of their own kind, other insects and other arthropods such as spiders and centipedes. They are certainly adapted to avoid and resist these, but the sensations and impulses which make up the hunting behaviour of an arthropod are difficult for us to appreciate, and protective measures directed against them equally so. Most of the protective adaptations which we can observe and study are those developed by insects against their vertebrate enemies, which have sensory equipment not unlike our own. Birds are the most important vertebrate enemies of insects and, like ourselves, they have sight as their dominant sense. The insects' adaptations for defence against them are accordingly easy for us to detect and understand, and much of what I shall have to say about how insects protect themselves will be in relation to birds.

In evolving their marvellously efficient bodily organization insects have had to pay one serious penalty; they are always small. Very few can put up a fight against attack by birds, and they are also at a disadvantage in running or flying for safety. Although dragonflies are masters of flight among insects, birds like bee-eaters and drongos have little difficulty in catching them, and flycatchers can cope easily with any sort of artful dodging resorted to by their prey. To escape predators that hunt by sight insects must hide.

Shelter

Vast numbers do this simply by burrowing or by creeping under debris and herbage or into crevices. During the day you can watch an area of soil or woodland mould and see no sign of the teeming population that lives just beneath it, though many of them come out and run about under cover of darkness. Sink a jampot to its rim in your garden, or better still in a wood, and you will most probably find flightless beetles and other small nocturnal prowlers in it in the morning, which have happened to wander over the few square centimetres of the trap and fall in.

Most of the heavy-bodied night flying moths (Noctuidae) that crowd into your Robinson light trap or onto your 'sugar patch', hide by day near the ground in long grass or under low-growing bushes like bramble and gorse. The more lightly built Geometrid moths (those with 'looper' caterpillars) mostly hide in a similar way in the foliage of bushes and trees. The few butterflies that hibernate as imagines also hide themselves away, the brimstone and comma in overwintering foliage, the peacock and tortoiseshell in hollow trees and outhouses.

Camouflage

Although most of these insects rely mainly on being under cover and so out of sight, we see among them the first stages of the type of adaptation commonly known as camouflage, but among biologists as cryptic adaptation or procrypsis. Turn an opened umbrella upside-down and shake into it some low-hanging leafy branches of a tree or bush. Numbers of insects will probably fall into it, beetles, bugs, lacewings, caterpillars, some of which will be brown but the majority green. Now collect loose leaf litter in a wood and shake or sift it over a white sheet. Again numbers of small insects will appear, all brown or blackish. Those sheltering in the live foliage inhabit a world of green leaves threaded with brown twigs; their situation conceals them well but in matters of life and death there is generally room for improvement. Many insectivorous animals turn over the leaf litter in their search for food; they find plenty of insects, but those best concealed by their colour have the best chance of survival.

The next stage in procrypsis is the disruptive pattern. This is the principle by which a military 'pill-box' can be made inconspicuous by dividing its surface into irregular areas and painting them in dark and light shades of green. The eye of the enemy will tend to see irregular shapes of no particular significance instead of the unavoidable rectangularity of a concrete structure. This principle is important in concealing large objects and animals whose outline is likely to betray them. In insects it is generally combined with resemblance to a particular background.

Before turning to the details of cryptic resemblance and simulation one other general principle has to be recognized, that of countershading, which is also more important in the concealment of large objects than of small ones. In the open air the chief source of light is overhead, so that any object tends to be strongly illuminated above and shadowed below, and the distribution over it of light and shade gives a great deal of visual assistance in determining its shape. A white disc stood on its edge and a white sphere of the same diameter are distinguishable only because the sphere is bright on top and shadowed below. If, however, the disc is painted pale grey and the sphere is painted white below, and carefully graded to grey of the same tone as the disc at its equator, and to darker grey above, the two will be indistinguishable when viewed horizontally. Most mammals, birds and fishes are coloured dark above and pale below to conceal their large rounded bodies. This countershading, as it is called, is not often seen in insects, but may be found in caterpillars that live in the open. The case of the eyed hawkmoth larva (*Smerinthus ocellata*) is of particular interest because the big green caterpillar is pale above and dark underneath. The countershading is effective because when at rest the

The caterpillar of the eyed hawkmoth demonstrates countershading adapted for an upside-down posture. The one on the right, with its back to the sky, is not in its natural posture.

larva hangs upside-down on the twigs of the sallow bushes on which it feeds.

At the art of self concealment by close resemblance to natural objects and backgrounds insects are unquestionably ahead of all other animals. Here their small size and their great diversity of form are advantages, enabling them to simulate leaves, green or withered, twigs, buds and even flowers, all of which are of such general occurrence that to resemble them is almost equivalent to possessing a ring or cloak of invisibility. The bark of trees and the lichen-grown surface of rocks are backgrounds of enormous aggregate extent, and many insects combine disruptive and imitative patterns to effect concealment when at rest upon them.

Hiding in this last way, on completely exposed surfaces, is a mode of procrypsis resorted to by a great many moths. Let us look at the one depicted on plate 7, a fairly large moth, the oak beauty *(Biston strataria)* which flies in Britain and over most of Europe in oak woods in early spring when the trees are still bare of leaves. Most of its visible area consists of the fore-wings, which form a flattened tent, covering the abdomen and sloping down from the thorax to the bark in a way that eliminates any shadow of the kind that would betray an upstanding object. The wings are marked and coloured to harmonize closely with an oak trunk with a sparse growth of lichen, and there is an irregular transverse black-and-white band which is strongly disruptive, breaking up the tell-tale symmetrical arrow-head shape. This bilateral symmetry is the one thing that cannot be quite concealed, and it is the clue for which the entomologist's eye must be alert when he is hunting for moths on tree trunks.

The oak beauty normally sits with its head higher than its tail, and it will be concealed whether upright or tilted. The pine hawk-moth *(Hyloicus pinastri)* rests on pine trunks in a strictly head-up position, thus aligning the dark streaks on its wings and thorax with the predominantly vertical fissures in the bark. The Geometrid moths mostly rest with their wings more extended, so that the hind-wings are exposed, and much flattened against the substratum. Some of these have a streaky pattern running across both pairs of wings at right angles to the axis of the body. Such species when resting on trees generally sit with the body horizontal so that their pattern is aligned with that of the bark.

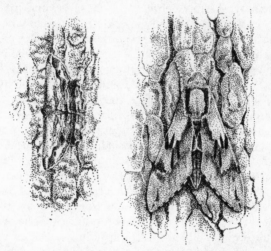

The waved umber (*Menophra abruptaria*) and the pine hawkmoth both rest by day on bark. In the hawkmoth the body is upright, in the Geometrid it is horizontal, so that in both cases the wing pattern conforms with vertical fissures in the bark.

An interesting experiment was performed on a North American Geometrid, *Melanolopha canadaria*. Moths were enclosed in a cylindrical chamber with a choice of horizontal or vertical black-and-white stripes to rest on, consisting of black tapes stuck on the white inside of the cylinder. The great majority came to rest with the transverse wing pattern disposed parallel to the stripes, whether horizontal or vertical, but with a slight preference for vertical stripes. If however the pattern of tapes was covered with a film of transparent cellulose acetate, so that there were no horizontal or vertical surface irregularities on the inside of the cylinder, the moths settled without any significant preference for aligning themselves with the pattern, showing that they made their choice of position by their sense of touch rather than of sight, and presumably also do so when settling on trees.

I mentioned rock surfaces as resting places. In parts of Scotland the grey mountain carpet *(Entephria caesiata)* can be found in large numbers by flapping the bag of a butterfly net against sheltered rock surfaces, causing the moths to fly off. You will discover twenty or more in this way for every one you can detect at rest.

The actual effectiveness of this sort of camouflage was demonstrated by H. B. D. Kettlewell in the course of his work on the peppered moth *(Biston betularia)* a close relative of the oak beauty. The moth is normally speckled black-and-white, but a wholly black form appeared in response to the blackening of bark near cities about the middle of the last century, when the Industrial Revolution was transforming the English Midlands. This has been interpreted as an unusually rapid example of evolution by natural selection, with bird predation as the selective agent. The two forms, speckled and black, now exist in Britain side by side, predominating in rural and urban areas respectively. In one of his experiments Dr Kettlewell chose an industrial wood near Birmingham in which 90 per cent of the naturally occurring moths were black, and an unpolluted wood in Dorset in which nearly 95 per cent were typical speckled. He bred large numbers of both forms and released them in each locality, marking each one with a dot of paint on the underside of the wing. A few days later he recaptured all he could in illuminated moth traps. In the Dorset wood the percentage recaptured of the total of released black moths was just half that of the speckled ones, and in the Birmingham wood the percentages were almost exactly reversed. Black moths resting on the lichen-covered trees in Dorset were found by their predators twice as readily as speckled ones, but on the soot-blackened trunks near Birmingham the pale black-and-white speckled ones were at an equal disadvantage. In another experiment he and Dr N. Tinbergen released black and speckled peppered moths onto trees in urban and unpolluted areas and actually watched and recorded the faster rate of elimination by birds of the moths resting on the 'wrong' backgrounds.

The most advanced stage in procrypsis is reached when it operates by close simulation of natural objects, such as leaves and
twigs, which are of no interest to predators. Here deception rather
than concealment is the principle involved, and examples of marvellously precise simulation are often found.

The stick caterpillars of the Geometrid moths are among the
most familiar. These larvae feed on the foliage of bushes and trees
and their bodies are coloured and patterned to look like twigs,
usually with a specific resemblance to those of their food plant.
When they are not walking or feeding the caterpillars adopt a rigid
pose, holding on with their two pairs of abdominal feet and laying
the anterior legs closely against the thoracic segments, so that no
limbs are apparent anywhere. The abdominal feet, at the hinder
end of the body, clasp a twig in such a way that the larva looks
exactly like another twig growing out of it.

A more unusual piece of twig simulation is displayed by the pupa
of the Malayan swallowtail butterfly *Chilasa clytia*. The pupa is
slung against a stem in the usual Papilionid way, but all the curves
that are a normal feature of swallowtail pupae are straightened out
and the hinder end is ventrally hollowed so that the false twig
appears to be growing out of the real one, not just attached to it.
The blunt spines in front all point forwards, looking like parallel
fibres at the end of a broken stick. Among imaginal Lepidoptera
the buff-tip moth *(Phalera bucephala)* looks like a short piece of
dry rotten stick, broken and detached. Both thorax and wing-tips
have yellowish patches simulating exposed wood, and between
them the wings, rolled round the body to form a cylinder, are
bark-grey.

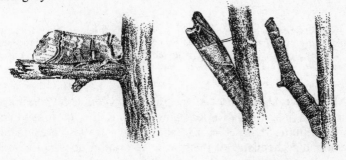

All three stages of butterflies and moths may be protected by looking like twigs.
Left, a buff-tip moth; *centre*, pupa of a Malaysian swallowtail, *Chilasa clytia*;
right, larva of the brimstone moth.

The tropical stick-insects are of course the professionals of stick and stem simulation. Both their bodies and legs are of a form requiring very little adaptation to look like green or brown plant stems, and many of them rest in postures so distorted as to relieve the animal of any semblance of an insect.

Imitation of leaves is carried to even more extraordinary lengths, especially among the tropical bush-crickets and leaf-insects. The primitively reticulate wing venation of both these groups is readily adapted to look like that of a leaf, and as the fore-wings are not used for flying (in the kinds that do fly), they can suffer modifications of shape to simulate leaves without embarrassing the insect in any way. In leaf-insects there are often expansions on the legs which look like small leaves. In both these and the bush-crickets green or brown dead leaves are simulated, and among the green species spots and irregular marks are often developed as specific characters on the wings, which convey an appearance of injury or fungus infection of a leaf.

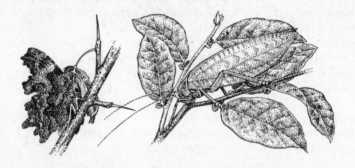

Many insects are effectively concealed by a resemblance to leaves. The hibernating comma butterfly (*left*) looks exactly like a brown, tattered, dead leaf. The large Sumatran bush-cricket is coloured bright green and is shaped to resemble a living leaf in a tropical environment of permanently green foliage.

Among the higher insects, the Endopterygota, only the Lepidoptera go in seriously for leaf simulation. Rather curiously they almost confine themselves to dead, brown leaves, presumably because the chemistry of their scale coloration does not readily provide green pigments. Butterflies, due to their resting posture, with wings closed over the back, can appear as either of two quite different creatures as the occasion demands. A comma butterfly

(Polygonia c-album), or one of its North American relatives the anglewings, is vividly conspicuous with its wings spread to advertise its identity to other commas. By closing them it changes abruptly, almost magically, into a dark brown tattered crumpled leaf with a small C-shaped crack in it through which the light seems to shine. The comma needs something special in the way of concealment, for the dead foliage among which it hibernates is a hunting ground of sharp-eyed birds all through the cold, hungry months of winter. The famous Indian leaf butterfly *(Kallima)* of tropical Asia closes its blue and orange wings to become an entire brown leaf complete with petiole and mid-rib, and here we see for the first time the phenomenon of coincident pattern. From the hind-wing tail, the petiole of the 'leaf', a dark line runs right across both wings to the tip of the fore-wing, forming a perfectly positioned mid-rib. But its continuity depends on the natural posture of the butterfly, for if the relative position of fore- and hindwings is not exactly correct the line is broken. The case of the Malayan moth *Enmonodia pudens* is more remarkable. Here a pale dead leaf is simulated, but the false mid-rib runs across the upperside of all four wings. Also the thorax is sharply divided, black in front, pale behind, and this has the effect of keeping the edge of the 'leaf' entire from one fore-wing base across to the other. When the moth is pinned and set in a collection the whole of this elaborate correlation is thrown out and the purpose of the pattern obscured.

It must not be supposed that insects which simulate leaves all look like each other. On the contrary they show an immense range of diversity. The 'leaf' may be green or brown or variegated, entire or torn or crumpled, of this shape or that. Birds which find one camouflaged insect are more likely to discover another identical one, and then more and more of them. They acquire what is known as a 'searching image', in more homely speech they get their eye in, so diversity is an essential part of the theme of hiding by deception.

One more mode of procrypsis is worth mentioning. It is in a way a curiosity, though of quite general occurrence, and it is exploited predominantly by the ever-versatile Lepidoptera. Birds are abundant wherever there is vegetation and the black-and-white splashes and smears of their droppings are often seen on leaves. What better means could there be of evading the appetite of birds than by imitating the appearance of their excrement? Quite a number of young caterpillars and small moths that rest among leaves are coloured and patterned in this way. Small size, a length

I.L.—F

or diameter of a centimetre or less, is essential, as bird droppings larger than this do not generally adhere to leaves. For this reason caterpillars of the larger moths and butterflies are only adapted to resemble the droppings in their earlier instars. When they approach full size they assume quite a different appearance. This is true of many of the swallowtail butterflies *(Papilio)*, both temperate and tropical species. In the alder moth *(Acronicta alni)* the young larvae are disguised as bird droppings, but the fully grown larva is conspicuously banded black and yellow and has long clubbed hairs. When breeding the moth it is noticeable that the young larva rests on the upper surface of the leaves but when mature it hides below them. Leaves are marked with bird droppings above but not below, so this is a case of adaptive appearance and behaviour being correlated.

Among adults moths many of the Tortricoidea resemble bird droppings, especially the species of the genus *Apotomis*. The lime-speck pug *(Eupithecia centaureata)* is another example of a moth protected in this way and affords a curious confirmation of the effectiveness of this device. When an illuminated moth trap is operated numbers of moths commonly settle on and around the trap, where they may be found by the energetic collector who goes out to his trap just before dawn. After sunrise they soon disappear down the throats of birds, which learn to attend the trap every morning. When there has been a large emergence of lime-speck pugs, however, they remain, very obvious to our eyes, sitting on the trap or on nearby walls and fences, until breakfast time and later, accompanied by no other moths whatever; the birds have picked all the others out but left the little white and brown pugs alone.

Safety in nastiness

From imitating something that cannot be eaten, the next step is actually to be inedible. In Europe, on hillsides especially of chalk and limestone, and on waste ground burnet moths (genus *Zygaena*) are often abundant. They are present in greatest variety in the lands bordering the Mediterranean, but range far to the north and east, and seven species extend to Britain. They are all brightly coloured with a red or red and white pattern on a dark background, and they are active by day, flying and sitting about on flowers in the sunshine. Nothing in their appearance or behaviour suggests any attempt at concealment, but birds disregard them, and with good reason. An aviary rook, without experience in seeking food in the wild, was once offered a burnet. It dismembered it and took the body into its mouth, but immediately dropped it and showed signs of acute distress, running round in circles, wiping its beak and copiously salivating. The greenish-yellow haemolymph or blood of burnet moths is intensely distasteful to birds and contains active poisons. Hydrocyanic acid is found in all stages, egg, larva, pupa and imago, and histamine is also present; a solution of the blood is fatal to small vertebrate animals when injected. In experiments of this kind it was found that a female containing eggs is much more poisonous than a spent female or a male. The moths themselves are resistant not only to their own poison but also to the hydrocyanic acid fumes of a cyanide killing bottle.

Their bright coloration and ostentatious behaviour renders them not only conspicuous but unmistakable, and this is to their advantage, since a bird, having tried to eat one, will have no difficulty in remembering their appearance and thereafter avoiding them. Young insectivorous birds must probably always learn by experience not to touch them since natural selection can only promote an inherited instinct by elimination of individuals which fail to act on it, and there is no reason to suppose that birds die as a result of pecking burnets. Many of the moths must therefore be fatally injured by birds, but their sacrifice saves the lives of many more, and the species gains protection. Adaptations advertising and warning against inedibility or danger in prospective victims of predation are called aposematic. This is a useful term because it includes shape, pattern and behaviour which the common expression 'warning coloration' does not.

Other familiar moths which are distasteful and have aposematic characteristics are the cinnabar *(Tyria jacobaeae)*, black and red not unlike the burnets, the tiger moths, especially the garden tiger *(Arctia caja)* and the magpie moth *(Abraxas grossulariata)*. When molested the garden tiger advances its forewings revealing the red black-spotted hind-wings, and also displays a strip of bright red hairs between the head and thorax. The magpie is a rather large Geometrid, white marked with black and yellow. Its larva has the unusual feature of being coloured similarly to the imago, and the pupa is black with conspicuous yellow bands. A moth pupa with any sort of adaptive coloration is unusual because they are nearly always hidden, but the magpie larva pupates in a thin transparent

The magpie moth is ill-tasting in all its stages, and is protected throughout by warning coloration; the larva and moth are white, black and yellow, and the pupa is black and yellow.

cocoon on the underside of leaves, through which the pupa is plainly visible. Birds are known to find the species distasteful and an eminent English entomologist has recorded that it has an unpleasant bitter flavour in all its stages.

No British butterflies are known to be protected by inedible qualities, but there are several mainly tropical Families whose larvae feed on poisonous plants, and the poison which they assimilate persists even through the organic upheaval of pupation into the body of the imago. The most widespread of these butterfly Families is the Danaidae whose larvae feed on milkweed (Asclepiadaceae) and allied plants. Many of these contain poisons called cardenolides which affect the heart-beat of vertebrate animals and may be fatal in heavy doses. Rather fortunately they are also powerfully emetic, at any rate to birds, and a bird which swallows a Danaid butterfly usually vomits almost immediately, voiding the dangerous poison and at the same time suffering enough discomfort to persuade it not to touch that sort of butterfly again. One of the few Danaids that extends beyond the tropics is the monarch or milkweed *(Danaus plexippus)*. It is a native of North America and a lot of research has been done on it in the United States, in the course of which the facts recorded above about Danaids were first established. In addition some other curious facts came to light. The birds used in the experiments were blue jays, and inexperienced aviary birds usually responded by being violently sick if they swallowed a monarch, and by recognizing and avoiding them thereafter. With great difficulty some monarch larvae were raised to maturity on cabbage and, as expected, inexperienced blue jays ate them without any ill effects.

But some monarchs caught in the wild were found not to upset the jays, and investigation revealed that some species of milkweed contain a great deal of poison, others rather less, others again little

PLATE 9. A leaf insect, *Phyllium bioculatum*, from Malaysia.

PLATE 10. **Warning pattern and behaviour.** *Above*, an eyed hawkmoth (*Smerinthus ocellata*) at rest; *below*, a moth that has received a 'peck' from a pencil point and has fallen to the ground. It is displaying the 'eyes' on the hind-wings, a performance that is effective in scaring away birds.

or none of it. As the larvae may feed on any of them it follows that wild birds may consume quite a number of monarchs in an area where a non-poisonous milkweed is prevalent. Sooner or later, however, an unwholesome one will be encountered, and it seems that the experience is so unpleasant that the birds take a long time to forget it, so that predation on monarchs is reduced although some of them may be edible. They all look alike, of course, and their tawny brown, black and white pattern is conspicuous and aposematic. In addition it was found that not all birds are equally affected. Quails will swallow monarch butterflies that have been bred on the most poisonous milkweeds and suffer no ill effects at all. No biological problem is ever as simple as it seems to be when first encountered. Other butterflies protected in a similar way are some of the tropical swallowtails, whose larvae feed on species of *Aristolochia*, and the tropical American Helioconiidae, whose food plant is members of the passion flower Family, Passifloraceae.

The first evolutionary step in these feeding habits may well have been the advantage the larvae gained by escaping accidental destruction by large grazing and browsing mammals, since these will learn to avoid ill-tasting or poisonous plants. Next the larvae would become impregnated with the poison, and finally a physiological process would evolve to preserve it to the insect's later stages. Aposematic characters, aimed at birds, would evolve at the same time.

Many caterpillars of moths are protected by a coat of hairs or an array of spines or bristles, which makes them uncomfortable to swallow. In some of the tussock moths (Lymantridae) the hairs on certain parts of the body are finely barbed and may be poisonous, and can cause serious irritation and inflammation of the skin. The Browntail *(Euproctis chrysorrhoea)* is one of these, and its larva should never be handled. Sometimes 'plagues' of these caterpillars occur on bushes at seaside resorts. They are brightly, aposematically, coloured and children handle them out of curiosity. Also the hairs from larval cast skins blow about and people with sensitive skins may develop acute urticaria. The processionary moths *(Thaumatopoea)* are found in continental Europe and Asia and are so called because the caterpillars travel between their communal webs and their feeding grounds in head-to-tail 'processions'. These, as well as bearing tufts of hairs, have a series of oval tubercles along the back which are normally concealed by lip-like folds. If the larva is alarmed the folds open and the tubercle projects. Its surface is covered with minute hollow hairs, each containing venom from a gland at their base. On the folds there are long branched hairs which move as the caterpillar crawls and brush the poisoned hairs off the tubercles, so that anyone touching the larva will receive them on his skin. They cause severe itching and inflammation, and in some oak woods in Germany notices are displayed: DANGER. PROCESSIONARY MOTHS. Most of these larvae have aposematic appearance and habits, the most obvious habit being gregariousness. When young they tend to live in communal webs and the older larvae remain close together, which increases their conspicuousness.

Defensive chemical warfare is widespread among other Orders of insects. Many of the bugs of the Heteroptera group emit a repulsive and characteristic smell and the shieldbugs (Pentatomidae) are often called by the alternative name 'stink bug'. Some of them are luridly coloured, often black and red, others, which seem to smell just as badly, are green or brown and quite inconspicuous. Here is a salutary reminder that entomologists cannot explain all the facts that they encounter.

There are many grasshoppers, particularly among the African species, which when alarmed produce quantities of evil-smelling froth from the joints of their bodies and legs. The bush grasshoppers *(Phymateus)* are of this kind; they are usually conspicuously coloured and when young, before they can fly, they crowd together in swarms which may travel for miles without disbanding. The swarm is always surrounded by an aura of the smell of their repugnant fluid, which combines with their warning coloration in repelling predators accustomed to feeding on ordinary grasshoppers.

The little beetles called ladybirds are attractive to us because they are slow moving and docile and prettily coloured. But they also have a strong unpleasant smell if roughly handled. This comes from their blood, which is leaked out through their joints, and they are refused as food by birds and small mammals. Their 'prettiness' is really aposematic, a warning not an adornment, and they do not hurry because they have no need to.

The big black bloody-nosed beetle *(Timarcha tenebricosa)* crawls conspicuously among the goose-grass on which it feeds. If molested it discharges its bright red blood from the joints around its mouthparts; the blood is caustic and repels predators.

Other beetles go further than this. Some of the American darkling beetles of the genus *Eleodes* assume a position as if they were
standing on their heads and spray a repellent liquid in the direction
of anything they take to be an enemy. The most astonishing
defence mechanism, perhaps of any insect, is that of the bombar-
dier beetles *(Brachinus)* which occur in various parts of the world.

Left, an American darkling beetle (*Eleodes*) that raises its tail and squirts a jet of
repellent liquid at its enemy. *Right*, the bombadier beetle ejects a boiling hot
explosive mixture to discourage an enemy pursuing it.

The British species has long been known to emit a miniature
explosion at its hinder end, and was, of course, named accordingly. The details of this piece of behaviour have been worked out
and are well worth recounting. Chemical substances called hydro-
quinones, together with hydrogen peroxide, are secreted into a
'reservoir' near the beetle's rear end, and this opens into a 'combustion chamber' which has a spout-like opening to the exterior.
When alarmed the beetle passes a quantity of the mixture into the
combustion chamber and at the same time releases into it catalytic
enzymes which cause the two to combine in a violent chemical
reaction. The products of this are water, oxygen and caustic
quinones. The reaction produces sufficient heat to vaporize part of
the liquid, causing the 'explosion', and the rest is blasted out in the
form of a boiling hot corrosive spray. When fully charged the
reservoir has enough reagents to produce from ten to twenty
discharges, and they must be most effective in discouraging pursuit.

Mimicry

When discussing the monarch butterfly I described the curious relationship between those whose larvae had fed on poisonous milkweeds and those which derived no poison from their food plant, and so were acceptable as food for birds. In a way the edible ones were taking advantage of the more usual inedible butterflies by gaining protection on account of the identical appearance of all of them.

The white admirals (genus *Limenitis*) are represented all round the temperate Northern Hemisphere by butterflies with the wings dark coloured and ornamented with white bands. The North American viceroy *(L. archippus)* is certainly a white admiral; its larva and pupa, the venation of its wings and other details leave no doubt of this. But in appearance it is so like a monarch that quite a close look is needed to distinguish the two species. In the experiments that I described with jays and monarchs the birds without experience of either butterfly ate viceroys without hesitation, but those that had suffered the unpleasant effects of eating a monarch almost always declined monarchs and viceroys alike. The other species of white admiral are preyed upon by birds in the wild, and there can be little doubt that the viceroy gains protection through its resemblance to the monarch.

This is of course a simple case of protective mimicry, a phenomenon first detected among the butterflies of the Amazon by the English entomologist H. W. Bates about 1860. In this context the genuinely inedible or dangerous animal is called the model, the deceiver the mimic, and the whole situation a mimetic association. The conditions needed for its success are a sufficiently close resemblance between mimic and model and the occurrence of both in the same localities at the same season. It will work best if the mimic is comparatively rare, otherwise too many members of the association tested by birds will be palatable.

Among tropical butterflies extraordinary complications are encountered in mimetic associations, which prove beyond all doubt that the resemblances are not a matter of chance, but as surely the consequence of natural selection as is the resemblance of a comma butterfly to a leaf. Frequently the male of a mimetic species has an appearance normal for its Family and genus, while the female closely resembles some inedible butterfly of another

Family, and looks nothing like the male at all. This helps to satisfy the rarity condition because it halves the number of mimics. It acts, of course, at the expense of the males, but the females' safety is of more importance to the species because they require a longer life in which to mature and lay all their eggs. Furthermore, female mimetic butterflies are often polymorphic, that is they appear in two or more distinct forms unconnected by intermediate forms, and each of these resembles a separate model. By this device the mimic can further increase its numbers because the models, comprising more than one species population, are rendered more numerous.

In the famous African mimetic swallowtail *Papilio dardanus* the male is cream coloured and black and has a tail on the hind wing. In Ethiopia and Madagascar both sexes conform to this pattern, but elsewhere in Africa only males do so. The female may be one of a number of forms, quite unlike the male and each other, which are without tails and which mimic distinct and dissimilar species of the inedible Families Danaidae and Acraeidae. The Malayan butterfly *Euripus nyctelius* is a Nymphalid, and the male looks rather like a small black-and-white purple emperor. There are two forms of the female, wholly unlike the male and mimics respectively of the male and female of the very common Danaid *Euploea diocletianus*, in which the sexes are dissimilar.

Mimetic association between two species of Malaysian butterflies, *Euripus nyctelius* (*top row*) and *Euploea diocletianus* (*below*). The male *Euripus* is in the centre and on each side of him are the two forms of the female which mimic respectively the male (*below left*) and the female (*below right*) of the ill-tasting model.

Another type of mimicry of a rather different kind was discovered, also in the Amazon region, by a German entomologist Johann Müller. In this area there is a great variety of inedible butterflies of the Families Heliconiidae, Ithomiidae and Danaidae, and Müller noticed that many of them resembled each other closely, even species from two of the Families or all three. He interpreted this by supposing that these species have, as it were, clubbed together so that young birds may have fewer lessons to learn, and images to remember, than they would if each species evolved its own distinct aposematic appearance. This of course will result in lower numbers of butterflies being killed and injured in the course of the birds' experimental hunting. The two types are called, after their discoverers, Batesian and Müllerian mimicry.

Clear-cut mimetic associations between species are better illustrated by butterflies than any other animals, but mimicry is very far from being confined to the Lepidoptera. Almost the only insects that can fight back against a vertebrate enemy are the formidable social Hymenoptera, the wasps and bees with their mass onslaught and venomous stings, and most of them are unpalatable to birds as well. In most regions where they occur wasps and bees each provide a model in a mimetic complex in which some of the examples are obvious and the rest less easy to define in a positive way.

In Britain there are six species of social wasps (*Vespula*) including the abundant common and German wasps and the hornet, *Vespa crabro*. These form a collective model for a number of mimics in their own and other insect Orders. An obvious one is the wasp beetle (*Clytus arietis*) with its clear black-and-yellow pattern, un-beetle-like jerky movements and openly diurnal behaviour. Others are moths of the clearwing Family (Sesiidae), especially the two hornet moths, *Sesia apiformis* and *Sphecia bembeciformis*; all the clearwings are day fliers. Some hover-flies are certainly wasp mimics, one of the most convincing being the large heath-dwelling *Sericomyia borealis*. The majority of hover-flies have a stripy pattern, usually black and some shade of yellow, but it is by no means always wasp-like, and some of these are too small to qualify as mimics of a Vespid wasp. Then what of the solitary digger wasps, some of which closely resemble Vespids? These are classified in a superfamily, the Sphecoidea, distinct from the Vespoidea and indicating a relationship with them as remote as that between the monarch and viceroy butterflies. Their stings are used for paralysing their small insect prey and are not formidable weapons. Little is known of their palatability and their resemblance to the social wasps could be explained as Batesian or Müllerian mimicry or as a case where both mimetic principles are operating together.

I have space to describe only one case of bee mimicry, that of the drone-fly, *Eristalis tenax*, one of the Syrphidae. This is a large dark brown hairy fly which very few people who are not naturalists will remove with their fingers when it is buzzing on a window pane, for fear of being stung. It has indeed deceived men since the dawn of history, and is the subject of the myth on which Samson based his famous riddle: 'Out of the strong came forth sweetness'. Samson had killed a lion and left the carcase to rot, and the people of his time believed that swarms of bees emerged from putrid carcases and could be expected to produce honey. The 'bees' are of course drone-flies whose larvae feed and grow and pupate in any sort of semi-liquid rottenness, and in due time the flies emerge in large numbers. The belief that they are bees, and could be engendered in this way, was not questioned until the 17th century and was finally disposed of in the 19th. People must surely have noticed that the 'bees' so produced could not sting and had only one pair of wings, but in those early times it was wise to ignore the evidence of your senses if it conflicted with tradition. Drone-flies are usually quite as common as honeybees. There is some evidence that they are distasteful to birds and that this is a case of Müllerian mimicry, requiring no difference in the abundance of mimic and model.

I have described examples of inedible beetles, one of them being the American darkling beetle *Eleodes*, which stands on its head and directs a spray of repellent liquid at an attacker. Beetles of two other genera are known, something like *Eleodes* to look at but with no chemical defence at all, which, when alarmed, just stick their tails up in the air. No doubt some animals, which have experienced the disgusting and corrosive discharge of the model, are persuaded to leave the mimic alone.

DISPERSAL AND MIGRATION

Dispersal is a necessity for successful species of animals and plants. It prevents local overcrowding and enables them to establish themselves in new habitats made available by climatic changes and other factors. It is more of a problem for plants because they are static, and adaptations for dispersal of seeds by wind and by birds and other animals are familiar to everyone. Most animals must achieve dispersal by whatever means of locomotion they possess, and flight is certainly the most efficient because it can traverse both land and sea. Of the flying insects the most widely dispersed are the small light-bodied forms such as aphids and the smallest flies and beetles. These are carried up by the rising air currents called thermals and then conveyed great distances by high-level winds. Research carried out with nets flown from kites, captive balloons and aeroplanes has shown that on a warm day the air from 300 to 1,500 m. carries vast numbers of light-bodied, weakly-flying insects which continue in diminishing numbers up to nearly 5,000 m. These may be carried great distances over land and sea, and their distribution as resident species is often determined by climatic zones rather than by the ocean and by the deserts and mountain ranges which are usually recognized as zoogeographical barriers. Not only winged insects are present in the aerial plankton, as it is called: newly hatched hairy caterpillars, such as that of the gypsy moth, have been taken by devices for sampling the plankton up to 600 m. above the ground.

This must be the gypsy moth's main means of dispersal since the females seldom fly, and the flight of the male can obviously have no bearing on the dispersal of his progeny. In the allied vapourer moths *(Orgyia)* the females are wingless and remain on their pupal cocoons, where they lay their eggs. Their young larvae are also beset with long hairs and could readily become airborne.

Although the aerial plankton consists of small insects, larger kinds may also be dispersed by the combination of thermals and strong persistent winds. There is no doubt that monarch butterflies occasionally cross the Atlantic in this way, and both the regular and occasional migrations of moths and butterflies from North Africa to Britain are without doubt assisted by southerly winds.

The bagworm moths (Family Psychidae) have wingless females which, after emerging from their pupae, await the winged males inside the protective cases in which the larvae live and pupate. The male fertilizes the female by inserting his abdomen into the case. In the common European species *Acanthopsyche atra* the fat grub-like females have been observed to drop to the ground, a few days after mating, where they are easily discovered and eaten by birds. In a carefully controlled experiment eleven of these fertilized females were fed to a captive robin and its droppings for the

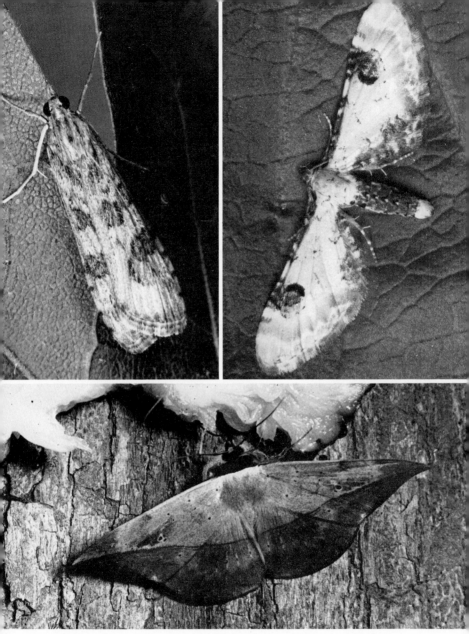

PLATE II. *Left*, rush veneer moth (*Nomophila noctuella*), a species that migrates to Britain from North Africa; *right*, lime-speck pug moth (*Eupithecia centaureata*) which is protected by its resemblance to a bird dropping; *below*, the Malaysian moth *Enmonodia pudens* feeding on a piece of pineapple. It illustrates coincident pattern.

PLATE 12. **Pollinating insects.** *Left*, the flower beetle, *Oedemera nobilis*; *right*, a small hover-fly, *Sphaerophoria scripta*; *below*, the large wasp-like hover-fly, *Sericomyia borealis*.

following 24 hours were collected and put in a special cage, where they were kept moist. After two weeks larvae of the moth began to hatch from eggs which had passed through the bird's body, and between 30 and 40 of them were recovered alive. It seems clear that the females' falling from the cases is a 'deliberate' offering of themselves for predation in order to secure dispersal for the species by a means more usually associated with berry-fruiting plants than with animals. As the larvae feed on grasses they are likely to find subsistence wherever they are deposited by a bird.

The term migration, when applied to insects, implies a regular seasonal movement of a species between two regions, sometimes but not always involving journeys in both directions. In the Northern Hemisphere movement is usually northward in spring, as conditions and availability of food improve in higher latitudes and heat and drought advance over the subtropics, and southward in the autumn. The red admiral *(Vanessa atalanta),* a common European butterfly, flies to Britain from the Mediterranean region in the spring. The females lay eggs on nettle and a late summer brood of red admirals is seen on our ivy bloom and michaelmas daisies. Unlike their relatives the peacock, comma and tortoiseshells these butterflies do not and cannot hibernate, but they have been observed flying southwards in the autumn. Some British red admirals probably reach a latitude where the climate permits them to breed, but there is no definite evidence of this. No red admiral ever flies both north and south as migratory birds do, the two journeys involve two successive generations.

Other butterflies that would never be seen in Britain but for seasonal northward migration are the painted lady *(Cynthia cardui)* and the clouded yellows of the genus *Colias*. None of these can survive a British winter in any of their stages, but both painted ladies and clouded yellows have been seen flying south in the autumn; as in the red admiral these are the progeny of the spring immigrants. The silver Y moth *(Autographa gamma)* is so abundant in Britain every summer that it is hard to believe it is not a resident species. It flies north from the subtropics in May and June, and in August and September there is another peak of abundance, partly progeny of the early migrants, partly renewed immigration. Great swarms of silver Y's have been seen on numerous occasions; from May to July these fly from the south, but from late August to October it is in the opposite direction.

The fact that quite small moths do fly to Britain from Africa was demonstrated dramatically in 1960 by Dr Kettlewell of peppered moth fame. In February of that year the French Government made tests of nuclear explosives in the Sahara. With great perspicacity Dr Kettlewell submitted all captures of migrants in his moth trap in Oxfordshire, subsequent to the tests, to a radiation detector, and in March he found a specimen of the rush veneer *(Nomophila noctuella)* containing a radio-active particle which could be identified with the explosion. Here was proof that the moth had actually performed the 2,500 km. flight from northern Africa to Britain.

The most spectacular and thoroughly documented butterfly migrant is that most instructive insect the North American monarch. Its pattern of migration is quite different from that of any of the European species, as individual butterflies make a long southward journey, hibernate in the subtropics and then fly at least part of the way north again. The butterfly is found in summer over the whole of the northern United States and southern Canada. In autumn those in the north collect together in groups and begin to move southward, and the groups may join up to form great swarms, flying rather high, 75 to 100 m. at about 30 km/h. They rest at night on trees and move south again next day. When they

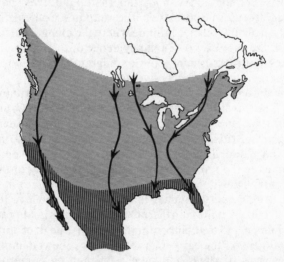

The monarch butterfly in North America. The shaded area shows the summer distribution, and the heavily hatched area superimposed on this shows the winter range within which the butterflies hibernate. Arrows indicate the main routes of the autumn migration.

reach Florida and the Gulf of Mexico in the east and Lower California in the west they settle on trees and pass the winter in a state of semi-hibernation; the same trees are resorted to year after year, which is remarkable since no monarch ever lives to hibernate more than once. Possibly their scent lingers on the chosen trees from one year to the next. In spring the butterflies gradually disperse and work their way north, the females laying eggs as they go. This migration is much less obvious and easy to observe than the autumn movement.

From eggs laid in the middle latitudes of the U.S.A. there are two or three generations before the return in the autumn, and those that reach Canada are likely to be children or grandchildren of the previous year's migrants. These produce a single generation of which the butterflies fly south in September. A Canadian monarch may fly nearly 3,000 km. southward and quite a long distance to the north before it dies. The practice of marking, releasing and recapture of butterflies, like the ringing of migratory birds, has contributed much to our knowledge about this migration. In Australia, where the monarch became established a little over a hundred years ago, a similar pattern of migration and hibernation has already been detected. It involves smaller distances and is, of course, reversed in direction and time of year since it is located south of the Equator.

Monarchs are occasionally seen in western Europe in autumn. It seems almost incredible that a butterfly can make the ocean crossing on its own wings, but in October 1968 at least 60 were seen in Britain and 9 captured. At the same time a number of North American birds were recorded, and this was a period of strong continuous south-westerly winds blowing across the Atlantic. There seems little doubt that these butterflies were derived from the rather high flying autumnal migratory stream along the American east coast and kept themselves air-borne long enough to be carried across.

The present world distribution of the monarch is of interest as an example of the migratory habit serving also as an effective agent of dispersal. The butterfly is undoubtedly indigenous to America and up to about 1840 was not known to exist as a resident species anywhere else. It was reported from New Zealand about that time, from Hawaii five years later and during the 1860s and 1870s became established in Australia. In the Indo-Pacific area it extended its range to include most of the Pacific islands, New

Guinea and parts of the Malay Archipelago. Eastwards from America it has become established in Bermuda, the Azores and the Canary Islands. There is no reason to suppose that man has transported the butterfly to any of these places. What he has done is to carry the milkweeds, on which the monarch feeds as a larva, to suitable climates all over the world, some accidentally, some as ornamental plants.

From prehistoric times up to a century and a half ago monarch butterflies were no doubt being carried away from their homeland over a great part of the world, supported by the winds and their own tremendous endurance. Most of these wanderers fell in the sea; those that made a landfall would feed and live for a time, but could leave no progeny for want of suitable food for their larvae. By sacrificing millions of its members on voyages like those of science fiction space-ships the species has at last been able to take advantage of man's meddling to make itself one of the most widely distributed butterflies known.

CHAPTER 3

SPECIAL RELATIONSHIPS AND WAYS OF LIFE

IN the last chapter I described various adaptations of insects designed to cope with the normal hazards of animal life. These include finding food and a mate, maintaining successful reproduction, protection from predatory enemies and dispersal to secure widespread establishment of the species and prevent local overcrowding. I shall turn now to some patterns of living that are largely or entirely peculiar to insects.

INSECTS AND FLOWERS

The central theme of this relationship is pollen. In primitive plants such as mosses and ferns fertilization of the ovum or egg is effected by sperms which swim in a film of water. The male fertilizing agent of the higher plants is the pollen grain. When one of these comes to rest on the female organ of a plant of its own species a tube grows down to the ovum and the male germ cell passes down it. Pollen grains have no power of movement of their own, but can be carried, by wind or other agencies, far greater distances than sperms can achieve, and so secure wider outbreeding and dispersal of genetic material. Pollen was first developed by the gymnosperms, the more primitive division of the seed-bearing plants, which are represented today chiefly by conifers. These are all trees or bushes, and they provide pollen which is always windborne, and this was probably its primitive mode of dispersal. The flowering plants or angiosperms first appear in the fossil record about the middle of the Cretaceous period, a hundred million years ago, when the dinosaurs were still flourishing, and they quickly became the dominant land plants. All angiosperms produce pollen.

For wind pollination to be effective pollen must be copious; many conifers produce it in enormous quantities. It is rich in nitrogen and proteins, and so biologically 'expensive'. By the same token it is excellent food for small animals, and insects must have discovered this very soon after plants first produced it. In feeding at male cones and at early flowers insects would often

97

carry grains of pollen from one plant to another. This would frequently result in fertilization, especially if the flowers were bisexual, having stamens and pistils present together. This is the condition in the majority of angiosperms, including some of the most primitive types such as magnolias, which are among the most ancient flowering plants in the fossil record. The amount of pollen eaten by the insects would be trivial compared to the colossal wastage involved in wind pollination, so an insect pollinated plant would gain two advantages: more secure cross-fertilization and production of seed, and an opportunity to economise in pollen production. The insects for their part would avail themselves of a valuable source of food. This, in greatly simplified terms is what we believe to be the opening chapter of the story of a sort of symbiosis on a vast and diversified scale, between insects and flowering plants. The account that follows of its development, leading to innumerable intricate adaptations both of insects and flowers must also be simplified and brief, and is best started by looking at the flowers.

One of the first developments concerns the pollen itself. In that of wind pollinated plants, both conifers and many angiosperms such as grasses and catkin-bearing trees, the grains have a smooth dry surface. Those of insect pollinated plants are often sculptured and ornamented and have a coating of oil, so that they clog together and do not blow away but adhere readily to insects which touch them. The oil may also make them more attractive as food. A second adaptation by the plants is the provision of nectar, as well as pollen, as a lure. This is simply a modification of the sugary sap, of which the plant has plenty to spare, presented in an attractive way.

If it is to compete successfully with other species for the attention of insects the plant must advertise. This, of course, is the origin and purpose of the bright, symmetrical structures which the word 'flower' immediately brings to our minds. At one time it was believed that the beauty of flowers was a gift of Providence for the delight of mankind, but there were flowers for many millions of years before there were people to admire them and some have 'colours' which our eyes cannot see. Their many coloured diversity is addressed, not to us, but to the insects together with which they evolved. This should serve to increase our delight in them, for the study of the intricate relationships between the insects and the flowers affords an intellectual treat fully as rich as the purely aesthetic admiration of them. Many flowers are deliciously scented too, and this is also primarily a lure addressed to insects, but a delight to our senses as well.

The shapes, colours and patterns of flowers serve first to attract the insects' notice, secondly to identify the plant (hence their unending diversity) and finally to guide the insect to the part of the flower where the nectar and pollen are to be found. It is to the advantage of a plant species if insects can be persuaded to go from one of its flowers to others of the same kind, rather than making random visits to various plants. The insect will also gain because plants of one species, flowering in a limited area, will all yield a copious nectar flow at the same time. Herein lies the need for each species to have readily recognizable flowers. Bees, which collect nectar and pollen in quantity, certainly do tend to confine themselves to a particular kind of plant on any one foraging expedition. Many kinds of flowers have lines or streaks converging on the position of the nectaries, or simply a distinctively coloured centre, like the bull's-eye of a target. The purpose of these is indicated by the term nectar-guides that has been given to them.

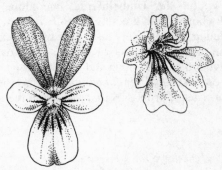

Flowers of pansy (*left*) and eyebright. The dark streaks, called nectar guides, show insects the way to the nectaries in the centre of the flower.

I mentioned in Chapter 1 that the vision of insects extends into the ultra-violet part of the spectrum, that is, insects see the ultra-violet components of sunlight as a colour invisible to us. Flowers could be expected, therefore, to be patterned in terms of ultra-violet as well as with colours that we can see, and indeed they are. This is easy to demonstrate by photographing the flowers in a darkened room illuminated with a strong source of ultra-violet light. All the flowers on Plate 3 are plain yellow to our eyes and are unpatterned if photographed in white light. In ultra-violet light (to which the emulsion on the film is sensitive) strongly contrasting patterns appear, either black bull's-eye centres or, in the case of the evening primrose, beautifully defined nectar-guides.

It seems likely that the earliest regular insect pollinators were beetles that fed on the pollen. The evolution of the important pollinating groups did not get under way until the flowering plants were well established, and it is a fact that beetles are the main or sole pollinators of some of the most primitive living angiosperms. These include the magnolia Family, the widespread tropical Annonaceae (custard-apple, breadfruit) and the water lilies. Soldier beetles (Cantharidae) are among the most conspicuous feeders at flowers with exposed nectaries. The handsome bronzy-green thick-legged flower beetle *(Oedemera nobilis)* belongs to a Family that feed as imagines only on nectar and pollen.

The insect groups that seem to have evolved side by side with the angiosperms are some of the more advanced flies (Diptera, Cyclorrapha), the Lepidoptera and the Aculeata or stinging Hymenoptera. Of all of them the bees have the closest relationship with flowers.

Many kinds of flies visit flowers with exposed nectaries such as ivy and the Umbelliferae, including omnivorous types like bluebottles and greenbottles *(Calliphora, Lucila)* and others that feed mainly or solely on nectar and pollen. Of these hover-flies are the most numerous and varied, and most of them have the usual higher flies' 'mopping and sucking' type of mouthparts. The common hover-fly *Rhingia campestris* has the mouthparts modified to form a stiff proboscis that can reach the nectar of tubular flowers.

Many flies are important pollinators. This peculiar hover-fly, *Rhingia campestris*, has a stiff proboscis with which it probes flowers for their nectar.

The bee-flies *(Bombyliidae)* are so called because they look very much like bees, and they are the most specialized flower feeders among the true flies. They have a long straight slender proboscis and take nectar from tubular flowers such as primroses.

The remarkable watch-spring proboscis of the Lepidoptera, the butterflies and moths, is a clear token of their evolution as feeders on nectar, and their fossil history, scanty and incomplete as it is, indicates that they were one of the latest insects Orders to evolve. Some Lepidoptera feed as imagines on the honeydew excretions of aphids, or on fruit juices; one genus is a blood-sucker and certain moths do not feed at all. A great many of them, however, subsist when adult on nectar, taking it from a variety of flowers, which are often adapted to attract either butterflies and diurnal moths, or moths that fly only at night. They are guided to the flowers by their senses of sight and smell, and the day-fliers certainly recognize colours. Blue, purple and violet strongly attract butterflies, which will sometimes fly down to blue artificial objects. Yellow is also attractive, but many yellow flowers reflect ultra-violet as well and in such cases it is probably this colour that the butterflies see. Most butterfly flowers, such as thistles, asters and scabious, are so constructed that they provide a firm platform for the butterfly to settle on.

Flowers that depend for pollination on night-flying moths are usually pale coloured and strongly scented. Some of the moths hover in front of flowers like jasmine, honeysuckle and tobacco which secrete their nectar at the base of a long tube, from the opening of which the anthers and stigmas project. The abundant

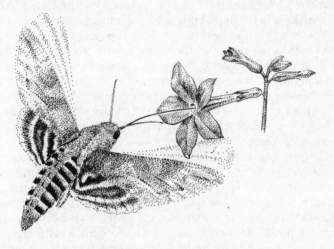

The big convolvulus hawkmoth hovers in front of flowers with very long corolla tubes ands uses its flexible proboscis to reach the nectar.

silver Y *(Autographa gamma)* feeds both by day and night and can easily be watched as it moves from bloom to bloom, never settling, and probes the flowers with its slender tongue. The most attractive and exciting of the hoverers are the hawk-moths. The little humming-bird hawk *(Macroglossa stellatarum)* is a day flier, and most naturalists are familiar with its beautifully controlled hovering and flitting from flower to flower among blooms of honeysuckle or valerian. It does indeed look very like a humming-bird, which are themselves important pollinators in their home in the New World. Some of the big nocturnal hawk-moths of the tropics have probosces of quite extraordinary length, up to 25 cm. The widespread migrant *Agrius convolvuli,* the convolvulus hawk, has a 12 cm. tongue.

The Hymenoptera includes the sawflies, ichneumon wasps, ants and the solitary and social wasps and bees. All visit flowers for food but the first three are of minor importance as pollinators. Social wasps feed in late summer on Umbelliferae and ivy in quite large numbers, and there are a few 'wasp-flowers', such as figworts and the helleborine orchids, which depend on wasps for pollination.

Bees, both the solitary and social kinds, can certainly be said to live symbiotically with flowering plants and must have evolved in close association with them. They are by far the most important pollinators in temperate climates and are almost entirely dependent on flowers for food, both as larvae and imagines. All solitary bees, other than the nest parasites, make stores of pollen moistened with honey on which the larvae subsist, and the social bees, the bumblebees and honeybees, store honey in cells or combs of wax and this, with pollen, is the basis of their diet throughout their lives. Note that honey is a substance produced from nectar by bees inside their bodies, differing chemically from nectar. Bees do not collect honey from flowers any more than we collect jam from gooseberry bushes.

When a small solitary bee such as the red Osmia *(Osmia rufa)* emerges in the spring from the cell made by her mother the previous year she first feeds on nectar and pollen and finds a mate. Then she searches for a hollow space of some kind with a small entrance, a hollow plant stem or sometimes a keyhole, and she is pleased to accept a piece of bamboo put out in the garden with the same motive as a nest-box for birds. First she collects clay and makes a smooth ending to the hollow. Then she visits flowers and imbibes nectar and also collects quantities of pollen in the dense mat of hair under her abdomen. These are mixed into a paste and piled up at the end of the hollow. As soon as there is enough to support the entire growth of one larva she lays an egg on it and builds a clay partition, leaving space for the larva to move in when it hatches. Another cell is stored and walled off with clay and then others until the space is filled and finally sealed with a plug of clay. There are many other kinds of solitary bees and some of them carry pollen to their nests entangled in hairs on their hind legs.

The economy of social bees will be described later in this chapter. They need to eat both nectar and pollen in quantity in order to produce the wax they use for building and predigested food for their larvae. As well as nectar for honey they take pollen home in beautifully designed 'pollen baskets' on their hind-legs, formed of curved bristles on each side of a hollow on the outer surface of the tibia. You will often see a worker bee with a yellow lump of pollen on each hind-leg.

Honeybees are effective pollinators of most flowers, including those of orchard fruit trees and some other commercial crops, but not all of them. Lucerne or alfalfa is grown on a large scale as fodder in North America, and it was found that, if honeybees were the only abundant pollinators of it, poor yields of seed result. Some small solitary bees were found to be much more efficient, and are now bred in millions in the vicinity of the alfalfa fields. Similarly bumblebees are by far the most efficient pollinators of red clover and, about 1880 they were introduced successfully to New Zealand, there being no native species there, to enable the growing of clover for seed. Bumblebees are useful and industrious insects but

Honeybees, as well as bumblebees, are sometimes 'nectar thieves'. This one is piercing the base of a bluebell flower and will obtain nectar without carrying any pollen.

are not always scrupulous in their quest for nectar. Some of them have rather short prosbosces which will not reach into tubular flowers, so they bite a hole at the base of the corolla tube and extract the nectar without coming into contact with the flower's reproductive organs at all. In this way they fail to fulfil their side of the age-old bargain between bees and flowers. Entomologists have a name for them – nectar thieves.

In the association between flowers and insects one might suppose that the insects would always play the active role, the flowers a passive one. This is usually the case, but there are exceptions; some flowers booby-trap or hoodwink their visitors. This may have the form of a harmless trick such as that played by the sage plants *(Salvia),* which are specialized for pollination by bees. In

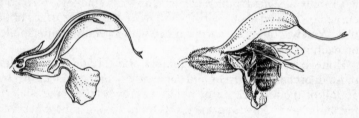

Two diagrams showing the pollination mechanism of the meadow sage *(Salvia pratensis).* See text for explanation.

this flower the stamens are hidden in the hood-like upper lip, and at the base they expand to form a plate that blocks the way to the nectar. The stamens are movable and pivot on a point just above the plate. When this is pushed into the flower by a bee the anthers swing down and hit the insect on the back, dusting it with pollen. At this early stage in the flower's development the forked stigma just projects from the hood and makes no contact with a visiting bee, but as the flower grows older its style lengthens, bringing the stigma down to a position where the back of a visiting bee will rub against it.

In lucerne there is what is described as an explosive mechanism. The stamens are borne on a thick stamen tube which is held under tension between the keel petals. The holding device is released by the first bee to push its way between them, and the tube and style spring up, striking the bee underneath. Honeybees seem to dislike this treatment and learn to avoid tripping the mechanism by probing for nectar between the keels, but of course this leads to com-

plete failure of pollination. Some of the smaller solitary bees which
visit the flowers freely and disregard the discomfort, are specially
cultured in order to secure satisfactory pollination of lucerne or
alfalfa. I shall return to this in the last chapter.

The common wild arum or lords-and-ladies has an inflorescence
consisting of an elongation of the stem called the spadix surrounded by a hood-like spathe. The flowers are tiny and situated
on the lower part of the spadix, the female ones are in a zone round
the base, a ring of sterile flowers just above them and above this the
male flowers. Above them again is a ring of stiff hairs whose tips
point downwards. The upper part of the spadix is club-shaped and
usually purple. The spathe unfolds at the top so the club is
exposed, but remains overlapped round the lower part of the
spadix, enclosing the flowers and the down-turned hairs in a
chamber, narrowly open just above them. The club gives out a
putrid smell which attracts certain insects, especially the tiny flies
called moth-flies.

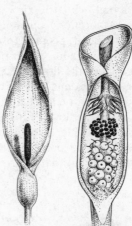

Left, an inflorescence of
lords-and-ladies (*Arum
maculatum*). *Right*, the lower
part cut away to show the male
and female flowers. See text for
explanation.

When the inflorescence first opens the female flowers are ready
for fertilization, the male flowers still small and undeveloped. The
flies cluster on the slippery club, fall down into the chamber past
the hairs and collect at the bottom round the female flowers; some
of them will be carrying pollen from another arum. The slippery
sides of the chamber and the downturned hairs prevent their
escape and they remain trapped for the night, feeding on droplets
of sweet liquid from the stigmas. By next morning the flower begins

to shrivel, the walls become rough and the obstructing hairs are limp, so the flies can climb out. But by this time the male flowers have masses of pollen with which the insects are thoroughly dusted on their way. None the wiser after their night of incarceration they fly to another newly opened inflorescence, taking pollen to the female flowers. Note that this elaborate device provides for almost certain cross-fertilization.

Orchids sometimes feature in science fiction, but the truth about them is quite as strange as the product of any writer's imagination. Although the tropical orchids display a fantastic range of size, form and colour, some of the small ground orchids of the north temperate regions are the most highly organized of all in their relations with pollinating insects.

The early purple orchid is a good example of these. It has a single anther on which the pollen grains are bound together by elastic threads to form a pair of club-shaped pollinia. These are joined by slender stalks to sticky discs, the viscidia, which are protected from contact with the air by a membranous pouch called the bursicle. At a touch from a visiting bee the bursicle ruptures and the insect's head, probing towards the nectar, is bound to touch one or both viscidia which immediately stick to it and become detached from the flower. Exposed to the air the viscid cement immediately hardens and the bee emerges with a pollinium, or a pair of pollinia, attached like horns to its head. Within half a minute of its leaving the flower further drying of the viscidia causes each pollinium to swing through an angle of 90° so that they point forward and are in just the right position to strike the sticky stigmas of the next orchid that is visited.

Head and thorax of a burnet moth (*Zygaena*) showing pollinia of the pyramidal orchid adhering to the proboscis. *Inset*, pollinia enlarged.

The pyramidal orchid is a butterfly and moth flower and its viscidium is single and saddle-shaped. On contact with a probing proboscis it wraps round it like a collar and the two pollinia are carried away on the insect's tongue. Burnet moths are often common where pyramidal orchids grow, and they can be found with one or several pairs of pollinia on their proboscis. The moth certainly suffers discomfort because it can neither curl its proboscis up nor insert its full length into another flower to feed.

The pollination mechanisms of the 'insect orchids' of the genus *Ophrys* are strangest of all. These are the orchids which resemble insects in appearance, the fly orchid, bee orchid and their allies. They were so named long before the resemblance was known to be anything but a coincidence, but it is now well established that the appearance and scent of these flowers deceive male insects into

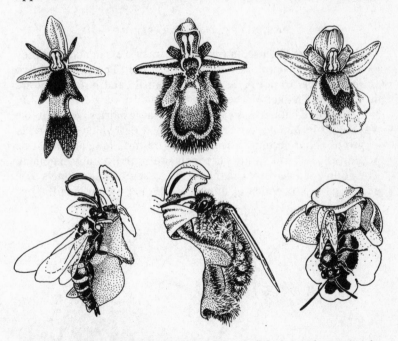

Flowers of (*left*) fly orchid, (*centre*) mirror-of-Venus (*Ophrys speculum*) and (*right*) yellow bee orchid (*O. lutea*); the two latter are found in southern Europe. The figures below show them being visited by insects which mistake them for females of their own species: solitary wasps, *Gorytes mystaceus* (on fly orchid) and *Camposcolia ciliata* (on mirror-of-Venus); and a solitary bee, *Andrena maculipes* on yellow bee orchid.

mistaking them for females of their own species. The males attempt to copulate with the flowers and the pollinia become attached to them in the process. The association is known as pseudocopulation, and is highly specific, as it must be since the sexual pheromone of any insect is peculiar to its own species and its scent is closely imitated by the orchid. The appearance simulation is, at any rate to our eyes, no more than approximate. Thus the fly orchid is pollinated by two closely allied species of the solitary wasp genus *Gorytes*; the remarkable mirror-of-Venus *(Ophrys speculum)* of the western Mediterranean region is visited only by males of a Scoliid wasp, *Campsoscolia ciliata.* Pseudocopulation is a strange freak of adaptation, involving exploitation of the insect by the orchid, rather than symbiosis, since the insect, considered as a species, derives no benefit from it.

PARASITES AND PARASITOIDS

Their small size fits insects well for a parasitic existence, and they have thoroughly exploited this mode of life. The fleas and two Orders of lice are all parasites of mammals and birds; they are described in Chapter 4. The curious Oriental earwig *Arixenia esau* is a parasite of bats, usually of the fairly large hairless bat, but one was found in Malaya on a wrinkle-lipped bat which has a body length of about 60 mm. The earwig is 25 mm. long and must be proportionately the largest ectoparasite found on any mammal. The notion of a flea or louse the size of a cat attached to one's own person gives some idea of how this little bat was afflicted.

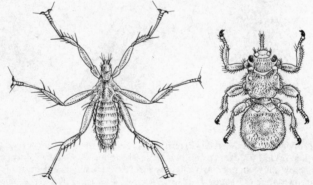

Wingless parasitic flies: *left*, a bat parasite (*Nycteribia*), *right*, the sheep ked (*Melophagus ovinus*).

A group of flies, known as the Pupipara, are external parasites of birds and mammals. The less specialized members of the group are winged and quite recognizable as flies; the forest fly *(Hippobosca equina)*, which lives on horses and cattle, is one of these. In the deer ked *(Lipopterna cervi)* both sexes are winged and fly strongly until they find a host; as soon as the fly has settled down among the hair of a deer it breaks its wings off. The sheep ked *(Melophagus ovinus)* never has any trace of wings and looks so unlike a fly that it is often confused with the sheep tick *(Ixodes ricinus)* which is an Arachnid.

These three species, with a great variety of others found both on mammals and birds, belong to the Family Hippoboscidae. The two other Families of Pupipara are exclusively parasites of bats. Some are winged, and fold their wings in pleats along the back when they are crawling in the host's fur. Others are wingless and look rather like six-legged spiders. All these flies reproduce in the manner described for the tsetse fly. A single larva grows to full size in the body of the female, which gives birth to it just before it pupates; evidently an imaginal diet of blood leads to this mode of reproduction. The mistaken notion that the fly gives birth to a pupa led to the term 'Pupipara'. It is not a natural group, the Hippoboscidae and the bat parasites having different evolutionary origins.

Among fly larvae there is an evolutionary sequence from feeders on carrion and those which develop in open wounds and as burrowers under the skin, to true internal parasites. Most of these belong to the family Oestridae, the bot-flies and warble-flies. These pass their larval life variously and disgustingly in the nasal cavities of mammals, in their stomachs and under the skin of the back, through which they burrow when fully fed and fall to the ground, where they pupate. The latter are the warble-flies, which cause serious damage by perforating hides destined for tanning and the production of leather.

For a successful parasite its host is like the goose that laid the golden eggs: the host must remain alive and as healthy as possible; if it dies the parasite is likely to perish as well. When one insect lives as a parasite of another, however, the relationship is usually a temporary one confined to the larval life of the parasite, at the end of which the host is killed. The life-history of the small ichneumon wasp *Apanteles glomeratus* will serve as an illustration. It lives as a larva in caterpillars, frequently choosing that of the large white butterfly, *Pieris brassicae*. The female wasp has an ovipositor with

Larvae of the ichneumon, *Apanteles glomeratus*, emerging from the body of a caterpillar of the large white butterfly.

which she pierces the caterpillar's skin to introduce her eggs. The larvae hatch and feed on the blood and fat of their victim, avoiding any of its vital organs. The growth of the host and parasites is completed at the same time so that when the caterpillar prepares for pupation on a wall or fence the fully fed ichneumon larvae bite their way out through its skin, killing it as they do so, and spin little yellow cocoons all round its remains. There may be a hundred or more of them.

Not only does the wasp spend only part of its life associated with the host, but the latter is doomed to a premature death from the moment when the eggs are implanted in it. Really this is a form of predation, with the death of the victim deferred to a convenient moment, and the special term 'parasitoid' is used for the insects which live in this way, though they are often referred to just as parasites.

The parasitoids are found among two Orders, the Hymenoptera and the Diptera. There are very few groups of insects that are not attacked by them and they are regarded as the most effective natural check on the multiplication of insect life. Manipulation of parasitoids is the basis of most attempts at biological control of harmful insects.

Among Hymenoptera there are two groups of ichneumon wasps, the Ichneumonidae and Braconidae and a third known as the Chalcid wasps or Chalcidoidea. The largest species are included among the Ichneumonidae and the most familiar of them are members of the genus *Ophion*, long-legged rusty-red or orange insects which fly at night and often come to artificial lights. Their most frequent victims are the larvae of fairly large moths. The Chalcids are all minute and include the smallest known insects, the fairy flies (Myrmaridae) which complete all their stages inside the eggs of other insects.

Apanteles, the parasitoid of the large white butterfly already mentioned, is a Braconid and has enemies of its own to cope with. Another small ichneumon wasp, *Hemiteles nanus* seeks out caterpillars containing *Apanteles* larvae and drives its ovipositor through the skin and tissues of the caterpillar into the little grubs developing inside it. If the yellow cocoons of *Apanteles* are collected from garden fences some of them are likely to yield *Hemiteles* wasps, which are secondary parasites or 'hyperparasites'. The story does not even end there: some tiny Chalcid wasps are parasitoids of *Hemiteles*, not secondary parasites but tertiary ones.

Quite fantastic situations arise out of hyperparasitism. The genus *Coccophagus* has been used in America to control a pest of Citrus trees, the black scale insect. Most hymenoptera, bees, wasps and ichneumons, have a peculiar method of sex determination. Eggs laid without fertilization always produce male insects, fertilized eggs produce females. The newly emerged, unmated *Coccophagus* female lays unfertilized male-producing eggs in scale-insects already parasitized by her own or closely allied species. After she has mated she changes her behaviour and lays eggs, destined to produce females, in unparasitized scales. These develop as primary parasitoids of the scale-insect, but the male is a hyperparasite on female parasitic larvae, often those of his own species.

Another extraordinary reproductive phenomenon that is found among some Chalcid wasps is polyembryony. The very small wasp *Litomastix* lays an egg in that of a moth, an insect very much larger than itself. The moth larva hatches with the minute egg inside it. Instead of developing into a single larva the Chalcid egg divides again and again, producing a mass of embryonic cells each of which develops into a larva. As many as 3,000 *Litomastix* wasps have emerged from one unhappy caterpillar of the American cabbage looper moth, but in this case several eggs were probably laid in the host egg. All the individuals arising from a single *Litomastix* egg are genetically identical and of the same sex, just as human identical twins are, and for the same reason.

The life histories of the ichneumons and Chalcids vary in every possible way. They may develop in the eggs of the host, be laid in the egg but develop in the larva, be laid in the larva and complete development before or after pupation of the host or, rather rarely, have all their development in the adult. Hardly any insects escape them. A wood-wasp larva, burrowing deeply in a pine trunk, would seem safe, but an ichneumon, *Rhyssa persuasoria*, the largest British species of the Family, uses its 35 mm-long ovipositor to bore through the solid wood and then slides an egg down it and into the larva's flesh. Exactly how the ichneumon locates her victim is still something of a mystery. The larva of *Rhyssa* does not live in the body of the wood-wasp larva. It holds on to its skin with its mouth-parts and sucks the blood. But when the big ichneumon larva matures its victim dies as surely as those of the internal parasites.

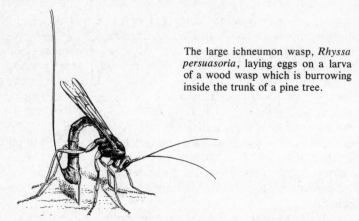

The large ichneumon wasp, *Rhyssa persuasoria*, laying eggs on a larva of a wood wasp which is burrowing inside the trunk of a pine tree.

Aquatic insects are far from immune. The eggs of the water-boatman are parasitized by a tiny Chalcid wasp which uses its wings to swim under water. An ichneumon, *Agriotypus armatus*, also enters the water to lay eggs in the encased larvae of caddis-flies.

The other important parasitoids are the flies of the Family Tachinidae. The adults are mostly rather bristly flies of undistinguished appearance, and their larval habits parallel those of the parasitic wasps just described, though none are small enough to be egg parasites. Their victims are mostly insects but also include spiders, woodlice and centipedes. Larvae of butterflies and moths are their most usual prey.

They have rather diverse modes of egg-laying, which can be divided into four categories. The eggs may be inserted into the host by means of an ovipositor; they may be attached to the skin or hairs of the victim; they may be laid on plants in such a way that they are likely to be eaten by caterpillars and then hatch in the host's alimentary canal; finally they may be laid in places frequented by a suitable host species and hatch into tiny active larvae which bore into any suitable creature they may encounter.

PLATE 13. Nesting of a solitary bee, *Osmia rufa*, in a piece of bamboo.
From top to bottom: bamboo split to show cells with clay partitions, pollen
stores and eggs; single cell with egg; single cell with young larva; single
cell with nearly mature larva.

PLATE 14. *Left*, an ichneumon wasp, *Ophion obscurus*: *right*, female earwig (*Forficula auricularia*) brooding her eggs; *below*, nest of a bumblebee, *Bombus agrorum*, uncovered by grass cutting.

The larvae of the wasp parasitoids appear to obtain enough oxygen for respiration from the blood of their host, and some Tachinid larvae also respire in this way. Others, especially in their later stages of growth, have to make contact with the air. Some connect their rear spiracles with the original opening which was made in the host's body. Others attach themselves to one of the larger tracheae of the host and use the air absorbed by it for their own respiration.

Tachinid flies are most often recognized when they appear in the breeding cages of lepidopterists. Any rather stout, hairy fly seen in the field may be one of them, and females have an obvious search-ing sort of behaviour when seeking for prey.

Cleptoparasites

With its meaning 'thief-parasite' this is the best term to apply to the bees and wasps whose breeding habits resemble those of a cuckoo. Indeed they are often called cuckoo bees and cuckoo wasps. Earlier in this chapter I described the nesting of the red osmia bee, with its series of cells each stored with pollen and serving as a nursery for a larval bee. The species of another genus of bees, *Andrena*, mostly make nests by burrowing in the ground. Each female digs a burrow from which brood cells lead off at intervals, and each of these is stocked with a mixture of pollen and honey which provides for the growth of a single larva. The bees of the genus *Nomada* are unusual in lacking any sort of pollen-collecting equipment such as an abdominal mat of hair or bristles on their legs. They are smooth-bodied and look much more like small black-and-yellow or brown-and-yellow wasps than bees. They have no need to collect pollen to sustain their offspring because they lay their eggs in the cells made by *Andrena* (and some other solitary bees) and their larvae consume both the food store and the eggs or larvae for whose benefit it was intended. The small shiny black and red bees of the genus *Sphecodes* are believed to live in the same way in nests of a genus of solitary bees called *Halictus*. Certainly some of them do, but some species may be honest gatherers of pollen. They all show at least vestiges of pollen collecting apparatus, an indication that their ancestors were normal hard working bees.

The nesting habits of solitary wasps parallel those of the bees quite closely, except that the wasps provision the cells in their nest with paralysed living prey on which the larvae feed. Spiders, caterpillars and various kinds of insects are hunted, stung to immobility and stored by the wasps, and each kind of wasp specializes in some particular type of victim. They too have their cleptoparasites, among them the brilliant little wasps of the Family Chrysidae. One of the commonest of these in Britain is the ruby-tail wasp *(Chrysis ignita)*, a metallic blue-green and crimson insect often seen running about on walls and fences. It lays eggs in the nests of solitary wasps and bees and its larvae feed on those of the host species and, if this is a wasp, on the store of food. It is really on the borderline between a cleptoparasite and an outright predator.

A ruby-tail wasp of the genus *Chrysis*, a cleptoparasite of solitary wasps and bees. The thorax is metallic green, the abdomen crimson.

The brilliant metallic colours of Chrysids fade after death; most young collectors of insects suffer this disappointment at some time or other. Their integument is very thick and strong and they can roll themselves up for protection against the stings of any house-holders who happen to be at home when they make their visits.

The 'velvet ants', really wasps of the Family Mutillidae, have winged males and wingless females, which do look rather like large brightly coloured furry ants. They lay eggs on the larvae of both wasps and bees after they have spun their cocoons, and their larvae feed as parasitoids. Female Mutillids sting severely and painfully and this has earned them the name 'cow-killers' in America. Needless to say this exaggerates the matter.

Galls

Plants that are attacked by parasites often respond by abnormal growth at the point where their tissues are invaded. The structure produced by this growth is called a gall. The formation and appearance of these galls are extremely diverse and almost always highly characteristic of the combination of plant and parasite that is involved. Some galls are caused by fungi, bacteria, eelworms or mites, but the greatest number are caused by insects, and only these will be considered here.

The principal gall-forming insects belong to three Orders, the Hymenoptera, the true flies or Diptera and the Hemiptera. Among the Hymenoptera the gall-wasps (superfamily Cynipoidea) are the most numerous and interesting. They are minute insects allied to the Chalcid wasps already described as parasites of other insects, and about 86 per cent of the large number of known species form galls on oaks and no other trees; their evolution must have been closely correlated with that of oaks.

In gall wasps the complete life cycle often comprises two generations, the individuals of each being quite distinct in appearance, habits and genetic constitution. This alternation of generations and other features of gall-wasp biology are well illustrated by the oak-apple which is caused by a Cynipid wasp called *Biorhiza pallida*.

Early in the year wingless females emerge from the soil below oak trees and crawl up their trunks. Without mating they lay eggs at the base of buds among the branches. The resultant gall begins to appear in May and rapidly swells during June and July to form a pinkish spongy mass about 25 to 40 mm. in diameter. This is the oak-apple, and inside it are a number of cells each of which normally contains a small larva of the *Biorhiza*. These larvae feed on the substance of the gall, pupate and the adult wasps make their way out through exit holes. They are of both sexes, which develop in separate oak-apples and normally have fully developed wings. The blackened and shrunken remains of the gall persist through the winter. Mating takes place in July after which the females make their way into the soil and lay eggs in the small roots of the oak. This also results in gall formation, the root-galls being round brownish objects about 7 to 8 mm. in diameter, and they often develop in groups coalesced together. Each of these contains a single larva which feeds in the gall for the rest of that year and the whole of the next, a total of 15 or 16 months. The adult wasps which leave the root galls about the end of the second winter are all wingless females and they start the cycle over again, each becoming the mother of broods either of male or female wasps.

Marble galls, often miscalled 'oak-apples', are found on small oaks in hedges and coppices. They are caused by a Cynipid called *Andricus kollari* which was introduced into south-western England about 1830 because the galls can be used for making ink and dyes. Each gall nourishes only a single larva, and during its life in the summer the gall is green. After the wasps emerge in September

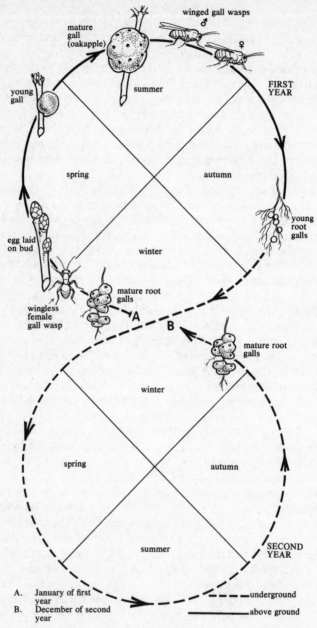

The life cycle of the oak-apple gall wasp, *Biorhiza pallida*.

and October the galls turn brown and persist through the winter as hard 'marbles', conspicuous on the leafless twigs and familiar to all country dwellers. The wasps from these galls are invariably females, and for many years the bisexual generation of *A. kollari* remained unknown, though it was suspected as long ago as 1882 that a gall-wasp causing galls in the axillary buds of Turkey oak *(Quercus cerris)* was really the other generation of the marble gall species. This has only been confirmed recently, establishing that *A. kollari* alternates between the two species of oak, *Quercus cerris* and *Q. robur*.

The spangle galls of oak leaves are something quite different in appearance; they are caused by Cynipid wasps of the genus *Neuroterus*. The common species *Neuroterus quercusbaccarum* causes little button-like discs to grow on the under surface of the leaves, often 50 to 100 to a leaf. They are yellowish-green in July but later turn to red, and each gall has the form of a short-stalked mushroom. In September they become detached from the leaves and fall to the ground. Each one contains a single larva which continues to grow after the galls have fallen and become covered by a carpet of dead leaves. In April wingless females emerge without any accompanying males, climb the trees and lay eggs among the young leaves and catkins. The galls that result in May and June look rather like red currants and are called currant galls. Male and female wasps emerge from them and the latter lay fertilized eggs on the leaves which give rise to spangle galls again.

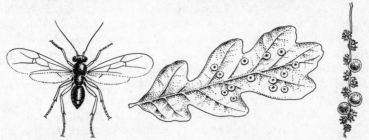

Three stages in the life cycle of a gall wasp, *Neuroterus quercusbaccarum*: the adult wasp, the spangle galls on an oak leaf and the early summer currant galls.

One of the gall-wasps that is not attached to oak is *Diplolepis rosae*, which causes the spectacular red hairy galls on wild rose known as the bedeguar gall or robin's pin-cushion. There is no alternation of generations here, and one generation a year, and the larvae overwinter in the galls. If these are gathered at the end of the winter and kept in glass jars their inhabitants may be bred out. It could be expected that these would be all of one kind, wasps of the species *Diplolepis rosae*, but this is far from being the case, in fact up to half-a-dozen insect species may appear as well as the primary causer. One of these is another gall-wasp which invades the gall as a kleptoparasite, having no power of causing a gall of its own. Both this and the *Diplolepis* larvae are attacked by parasitoids including an ichneumon and a Chalcid, and the ichneumon larva is the victim of a hyperparasite, another kind of Chalcid. The kleptoparasite, whose name is *Periclistius brandtii* (I will refrain from naming all the rest) also suffers from a Chalcid, whose larva behaves as an outright predator, devouring one thief-parasite larva after another, to the advantage, one supposes, of the larva to whom the gall already belongs. Most large galls are microcosms of this kind, and this is why I spoke of the oak-apple 'normally' containing larvae of its primary causer. It too shelters a small fauna of other insects. Entomologists with the skill and patience to preserve and identify these tiny insects have at their disposal an endless field for research, for there is much that is still unknown about these strange minute communities.

The sawflies, also Hymenoptera, are much larger insects than the gall-wasps. Their larvae are all plant feeders, but only a few of them give rise to galls. One example of these will suffice, the bean-gall saw-fly (*Pontania proxima*). The eggs are laid in the leaf-buds of willows and the larvae live in rounded red galls on the leaves, up to six or seven on a leaf. They do not look much like beans and the English name is ill-chosen and confusing. When fully fed the larva leaves the gall and pupates in a cocoon on the bark or in the soil. They are much parasitized by an ichneumon wasp. Males of this species are rare and most larvae are produced parthenogenetically, that is without fertilization of the egg.

Most of the gall-forming flies (Diptera) belong to the Family Cecidomyidae or gall-midges. Lime or linden trees are attacked by several of these tiny flies. *Dasyneura tiliamvolens* causes the edge of the leaf to roll over the upper surface and the affected part of the leaf turns purplish-brown. *Contarinia tiliarum* makes a gall at the end of the leaf petiole, just below the blade. These galls are easy to find as they are commonest among the young shoots that rise from the trunk, and when mature they are rounded and bright red; the affected leaf becomes stunted and hairy. The strange developmental abnormalities seen among the gall-wasps are not a feature of gall-midge life histories.

A number of galls are caused by aphids, which belong to the Hemiptera. One of these, *Pemphigus bursarius* is responsible for purse galls on the petioles and midribs of the leaves of the black or Lombardy poplar. The gall is initiated by an unmated wingless female hatched from an over-wintered egg. She pierces the petiole to suck the juices and at this point a gall forms which encloses her completely. Inside it she feeds and reproduces, and her winged offspring escape through a characteristic beak-like opening in the gall. These, all females, fly to sow-thistle and lettuce plants where they feed on the roots, but without producing galls. They multiply, still asexually, and then return to the poplars and in the autumn a generation arises of males and females which produce fertilized eggs that overwinter on the bark and hatch in the spring to renew the cycle.

SOCIAL INSECTS

This term is used to describe the ants and termites, and some of the bees and wasps, which live in organized communities. Many insects are gregarious, moving about in swarms like locusts or resting or hibernating crowded together. Examples of this are offered by overwintering ladybirds and by the caterpillars of lackey or webworm moths, browntail moths and others. These are poisonous or distasteful insects, and the gregarious habit enhances their repellent quality. There is, however, little or no behavioural intercourse between them, and the habit persists for only part of their life cycle.

True social behaviour in insects appears to have arisen from a progressive development of maternal care, resulting in a social unit based on the mother and her offspring. Brief and simple parental care is encountered here and there among several Orders of insects. The female parent bug *(Elasmucha grisea)* lays a compact batch of 30 to 40 eggs on a birch leaf and covers them with her body for two to three weeks until they hatch. She continues to brood the young and after their first ecdysis she moves about and they follow her for a time. The whole performance strongly recalls a hen with a nest and a brood of chicks. The female earwig lays eggs in a small hollow under a stone, and her behaviour is of much the same kind. In both cases the eggs will not hatch if they are parted from the mother insect.

Two orange and black sexton beetles preparing to bury a dead mole.

A rather less rudimentary sort of family life is seen in some beetles, including the dung beetles or scarabs. In one of these, *Geotrupes typhoeus*, the male and female cooperate in digging a deep burrow in which they live and breed, storing dung as food for the larvae. The female stays with the young for most of their development. In some of the scarabs which roll balls of dung before burying it both parents inhabit the burrow until the young beetles of the next generation are ready to leave it. The sexton or burying beetles *(Necrophorus)* bury small animals to provide food for themselves and their larvae. The male and female work and feed together during the interment, but the male leaves after mating. The female stays until her eggs hatch and then feeds the young larvae with regurgitated liquid food, leaving only when they are large and strong enough to feed themselves. The tropical beetles of the Family Passalidae live under loose bark in family groups in which male and female are associated with a number of larvae, which they feed with chewed-up wood. Both adults and larvae stridulate and it is suggested that the sound so produced helps to keep the group together. Versatile as the beetles are, this is as far as they have ever progressed towards living in communities.

Both their climatic distribution and their habits make the social Hymenoptera more familiar than the mainly tropical termites, and also they include many non-social species which show a gradation from simple parental care towards life in communities. Among the so-called solitary wasps the females confine themselves in most cases to providing food and a sheltered home for the development of their larvae, but this provision is often carried to elaborate lengths. The normal pattern is for the wasp to make a nest of some sort, which may or may not be divided into compartments. She may burrow into the ground, seek out hollow stems or disused burrows in wood, or build a structure of wet, quickly hardening mud. These reach their highest development in the elegant undivided nests of the potter-wasps *(Eumenes)*, each of which shelters a single larva. Confining itself to a class of victims particular to its own species, the female wasp hunts caterpillars, spiders or some special kind of insect. These are stung so that they are paralysed (let us hope that they are anaesthetized as well) and packed into the cells (or single compartment) of the nest, and a single egg is laid in each cell. The larva that hatches eats its victims alive and is thus assured of fresh unspoiled food throughout its life; just enough victims are provided for the completion of its growth.

Usually the mother wasp closes up her completed nest and has no contact with her offspring beyond the egg stage. Research in Holland has made one solitary wasp, *Ammophila pubescens*, famous for going beyond this stage of parental care. It is one of the digger wasps (Sphecidae) and the female makes single-chamber nests in burrows, and continues to visit them after each has been provided with an egg and a paralysed caterpillar. Furthermore she maintains several nests in different stages and needing different sorts of attention. In one that is inspected the egg may not have hatched. In another there is a small, or a large, wasp larva, and she will bring during the day one to three caterpillars to the former, or as many as seven to the large one. In another nest the larva may have completed its growth so that the nest stands in need of final closure. She makes a morning inspection of all the nests and this determines how she treats them for the rest of the day. If caterpillars are added to or removed from nests by a human observer, this makes no difference to the routine determined by the inspection in the morning, but even so she performs a feat of memory and coordinated action that one would admire in many 'higher' animals. This is clearly a step in the direction of sociality, limited by the fact that the life span of the mother is too short to overlap that of any of her daughters.

Another digger wasp, *Cerceris rubida*, studied in Italy, goes a step further. Towards the end of the season its nests may contain an old mother and four or five daughters, all living together and taking turns in guarding the nest entrance. Male Hymenoptera never seem to have any role to play in their species' life cycle beyond impregnation of the females.

Let us now turn to the solitary bees. As already described for

Osmia rufa, they have nesting habits that run parallel to those of the solitary wasps, except that the bees never display the beautiful versatility of the wasps in making mud nests; and, of course, they provision their nests with pollen and honey.

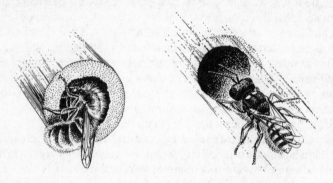

A solitary bee, *Osmia rufa*, and a solitary wasp, *Ectemnius cavifrons*, each at the entrance of its nesting hole. The bee is nesting in a piece of bamboo and the wasp in a hole bored in a dead log.

Thirty-six species of *Halictus* are found in Britain, a much greater number in the United States and a vast number of species all over the world. They are mostly small bees, blackish in colour and the species are difficult to separate, and this has hindered research into their habits. Some are ordinary solitary bees in which fertilized females, having survived the winter in hibernation, make separate nests in the spring, provisioning the cells in the usual way. From these a generation of males and females appear in summer of which the males die soon after mating and the females go into hibernation. In some species the spring female may survive long enough to be present in the nest when the summer females, her daughters, are emerging. Even if mother and offspring do not cooperate in any way, here is the first hint of social behaviour.

A real social organization, on a very small scale, is seen in a group of species which includes the British *Halictus calceatus*. The spring females, which have hibernated, make a nest and produce offspring which are all female. These may or may not be different externally from their mother, but they remain unmated (there being no males so early in the year) and their ovaries do not develop fully. They are essentially worker bees. They do all the work of the summer nest and the old spring female assumes the role of 'queen', remaining in the nest and laying most of the eggs that produce another, autumn, brood of males and females. Some of the males may develop from unfertilized eggs laid by the workers. The males of the autumn brood mate and then die and the females go into hibernation. The number of workers is very small, from about six to ten, but these species of *Halictus* conform to the definition of a social insect as one in which adult females undertake the care of larvae which are not their own offspring.

In some species, such as *Halictus maculatus,* several spring females may construct separate nests with a common entrance burrow. Here observation of the entrance alone gives a false impression of one large colony rather than several smaller ones.

When on the subject of reproduction I described the peculiar mode of sex determination in the Hymenoptera: fertilized eggs produce female offspring, unfertilized ones produce males. This principle operates in the curious alternation of unisexual and bisexual generations in the gall-wasps, and in the higher Hymenoptera it can be controlled, apparently at will, by the impregnated female. This has certainly been an important factor in enabling the Hymenoptera to evolve repeatedly and successfully as social animals, since it gives them a means of population control which can readily be applied when and where it is needed. King Solomon suggested that we should look to the ant as a model of industry, but this other lesson that they have for us is a much more important one. Bees, wasps and ants have been successful social animals for millions of years, far more successful than we are after a few thousand years (and only two or three hundred generations) of living in populous communities, and this fact is now becoming more apparent with every passing decade of human history.

After this rather sombre digression let us return to entomology and consider the *Polistes* wasps. This is one very widespread genus of the Family Vespidae or paper wasps, which are all truly social insects and make more or less elaborate nests by chewing wood to a paste and using this as building material. The behaviour of the various species of *Polistes* is easy to observe because the nest is small, suspended above the ground and open without any envelope surrounding and concealing the cells or comb, as these are collectively called. Also these wasps are found in tropical and warm-temperate climates all over the world, so that many entomologists have had access to them. Unfortunately their distribution just stops short of the British Isles.

The nest usually has the form of an inverted saucer, hanging by a stalk and containing a comb of hexagonal cells all opening downwards. The number of cells in most of the European species is less than a hundred. The wasps attending a nest all look alike, but they can be caught and marked with different coloured paints, so that the behaviour of individuals can be observed, and it will be found that one of them stays on the nest and does all or most of the egg-laying. She is the queen and the rest, on average a little smaller but not positively distinguishable from her, are the workers. They forage for food, caterpillars and insects of various kinds, which they chew up and give to the queen and to the larvae in the comb. They also collect wood pulp to enlarge and repair the nest.

Early in the season small nests of a dozen cells or less can be found with one wasp, the queen, on guard. She will have hibernated and, on emergence in the spring, will have constructed the little nest on her own. In the autumn some of the wasps on the comb are noticeably inactive and stay on the nest. These are the young queens which will hibernate after mating. If the queen is removed or accidentally lost the workers will lay eggs in the cells and these, being unfertilized, produce males. Probably many of these originate naturally from nests in which the queen dies early.

The habits of the common species *Polistes gallicus* vary in different parts of its range. In northern localities the development of the nest is as I have described, but in Italy it has been observed that nests are usually founded by three or four queens together. After it is established one of them becomes dominant, attacking and harassing the others so that they disappear. In another species

A queen of the paper wasp (*Polistes gallicus*) on her nest early in the breeding season.

one of the auxiliary foundresses has been observed to start laying
eggs in competition with the queen. An unedifying contest follows
in which each one eats the other's eggs and replaces them with her
own. The one which eats and lays more vigorously establishes
herself as queen. When a number of foundresses are inhabiting a
nest a dominance heirarchy or 'pecking order' is established
among them, with the eventual queen at its head.

A *Polistes* nest starts as a tiny stalactite of wood pulp and the
first cell built from it is round. As soon as others are built around it,
it becomes hexagonal in section, and all cells in the comb are
hexagonal when they are surrounded by other cells, each having an
equal contact with six of its neighbours. Unshared cell sides,
around the edge of the nest, are circular in outline. All the comb-
making social wasps and bees make hexagonal cells, and they can
be seen to use their antennae like dividers or callipers when they
are at work.

The familiar British social wasps belong to the genus *Vespula*,
there being several species of which two are equally common and
very similar. These are the common wasp *(V. vulgaris)* and the
German wasp *(V. germanica)*, both of which usually make paper
nests underground, though in recent years they have taken to using
the wooden nest-boxes provided for birds. In North America the
yellow-jackets and the bald-faced hornet are also species of
Vespula. The yearly breeding cycle is much like that of the more
northern kinds of *Polistes*, but the single queen is considerably
larger than the workers and differently marked as well so that she is

A queen of the common wasp on
a nest that she has made hanging
from the roof of a bird nesting
box; no workers have been
produced at this stage.

always distinguishable. The nests are much bigger and worker populations far larger. In the summer a common wasp's nest may have as many as 3,000 workers in it; the total number of the queen's offspring that hatch, live and die in the service of the nest during a season is probably five times that number.

A *Vespula* nest starts like that of a *Polistes,* with a little pillar hanging from a root (or a branch if the nest is above ground) onto which a cell is built and then more cells forming a small comb. The queen then makes dome-shaped covers or envelopes, attached around the base of the pillar and surrounding the cells. Two to four of these are made with air spaces between them and openings at the bottom, and they provide effective heat insulation. The nest made by the queen is six or seven centimetres across, and in it she lays eggs and brings up a small brood of workers. These and their sisters, which quickly follow, take over all the work of the nest, enlarging it, feeding the larvae and the queen and defending it with their stings. When the nest is complete it is as big as a football, a hollow sphere with a layered, spongy paper covering. It contains from six to ten horizontal combs that extend right across it, joined and supported by little struts or pillars of paper. The nest maintains this form, with the combs increasing in number, throughout its construction. The walls increase only slightly in thickness, they are never breached, nor are the storeys of cells partitioned. Both inside and out the nest seems to grow like a fruit on a tree, yet it has been built in as literal a sense as a house is built by bricklayers, but on an entirely different principle. All through the period of enlargement the inside of the nest is continually being nibbled away and re-pulped, to be added, together with fresh pulp, to the outside and to the new expanding tiers of cells. In the case of the underground nests there is continual excavation and enlargement of the hole under the root to which the queen originally attached the nest, and a space is maintained below it to act as a midden into which falls all the accumulation of excrement, dead wasps and larvae and inedible parts of prey, the rubbish and litter that is inseparable from a social existence. I referred in a previous chapter to the hoverflies whose larvae live as scavengers in wasp middens, ignored by the wasps which spare no caterpillars and insects that they can find and catch in the surrounding countryside and bring home as food for their larvae.

The temperature in the nest is kept warm and constant at around 30°C. Heat is supplied by the metabolism of the larvae and the wasps living in it. When nests are established in bird-boxes they tend to heat up on sunny days. At such times it can be seen that every worker, as she leaves the nest, stands at the entrance facing outward and buzzes for a few seconds before flying. By doing so she fans a current of air back into the nest, cooling and ventilating it.

Towards the end of the life of the colony the workers start building larger cells, and the larvae from the eggs laid in them develop into the queens of the next generation. At the same time males appear in the nest, coming from both large cells and small ones. Queen cells of this sort are never found in *Polistes* nests.

In temperate regions only impregnated queens survive the winter and nests are always founded by a single queen. The nest of the tropical social wasps and hornets may persist for years and new nests are founded by swarming in the way made familiar by honeybees. Wasps of the genus *Polybia* have been studied in Brazil and it has been claimed that colonies of one species may persist for 25 years; they certainly remain for three or four, in spite of the constant danger of attack by driver ants. The swarms that leave the more populous nests consist of young fertilized queens accompanied by numerous workers, which build a substantial nest before the queen starts laying eggs.

BUMBLEBEES

Having left the bees at the very primitive social stage seen in *Halictus* we turn now to the bumblebees, whose state of civilization is comparable with that of *Polistes,* but their architecture far behind that of the wasps. The annual cycle is the now familiar one of impregnated females emerging in the spring from hibernation and founding nests in which the work is done later on by their industrious but sterile daughters. The production and use of wax for building cells and comb is very characteristic of the fully social bees and the bumblebees' use of it is simple and primitive. It is secreted from between the segments of the abdomen, and a lot of nectar and pollen is eaten by the bees in order to produce it.

In the northern temperate climates where they have been most studied the great majority of bumblebee queens seek out an abandoned nest of a mouse or a vole and use the chewed and shredded grass and roots as nesting material, which they seem unable to prepare for themselves. Having found her mouse's nest the queen pushes out a chamber in it, dries it for a day or two with the warmth of her body and them makes a shallow cup of wax on the floor. Then she goes out foraging and brings home pollen which is moistened with honey and packed into the cup; a number of eggs are laid on it and it is then covered wax. The second wax structure the queen makes is a little pot in which she keeps honey as a food store for herself in bad weather. After a few days the eggs in the sealed cell hatch and the larvae start to feed on the pollen that forms the floor of their nursery. This is soon finished and their mother then feeds them by biting a hole in the wax of their cell and injecting a mixture of honey and pollen with her proboscis. As the larvae grow the queen alters and adds to their cell so that it keeps pace with their growth.

In about a week the larvae are fully grown and they spin cocoons and pupate, thus occupying separate compartments for the first time. About this time the queen starts making additional egg-cells with pollen floors, attached to the outside of the irregularly shaped bundle of cocoons. Wax from the first much enlarged cell is chewed up and 'recycled' in making the new egg-cells. The first young bees appear rather over three weeks after the eggs were laid, and their mother helps them to bite their way out of their cocoons. They feed from the honey-pot and in two or three days are strong enough to go out and collect nectar and pollen. The queen may continue to go out, but as soon as there are enough workers she stays in the nest for the rest of the season. She goes on laying eggs in little wax pockets attached to the sides of the cocoons and feeding and incubating the brood, fed herself by her devoted daughters. A large colony may reach a total of 400 bees, but around 150 is more usual. Males and new queens are produced in the usual way towards the end of the season; larvae destined to become queens are fed more generously and grow larger than worker larvae. By this time the queen has altered greatly in appearance; her wings are tattered and most of the fur is worn off her body; which is black and shiny. At the end she and a few aged workers are left sitting about on the decaying and parasite-ridden comb, and there they die.

This is a description of the economy of one sort of bumblebee nest, there are specific variations in the mode of feeding of the larvae and also in the situation of the nest. Some species nest in burrows previously tenanted by mice, others in mouse nests on the ground among the grass roots. Of all social bees and wasps the bumblebees make the least tidy nests; so far from being compar-

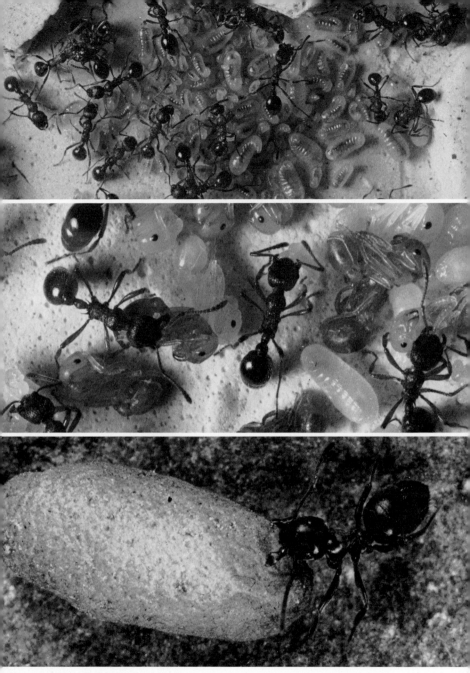

PLATE 15. **Ants.** *Above*, red ants (*Myrmica ruginodis*), workers with small and large larvae; *centre*, the same species with pupae, a few larvae and one ant (lower left) carrying a bundle of eggs. These are typical exarate pupae, and the ants are in a plaster nest or formicarium. *Below*, a black ant worker (*Lasius niger*) dragging along a queen cocoon.

PLATE 16. **Primitive insects.** *Above*, marine springtails (*Anurida maritima*); *left*, a mayfly, *Cloëon dipterum*; *right*, *Campodea* sp., Order Diplura.

able with a city, like the teeming colonies of honeybees and ants, a bumblebee nest has an endearing quality of domesticity about it, like an overcrowded one-roomed cottage. They are attractive in their appearance and their rather clumsy buzzing and scrambling among the garden flowers, and they are valuable pollinators, working longer and later hours than honeybees. They can sting but only do so under strong provocation.

The term 'cuckoo-bee' is used to describe the nest parasites of solitary bees. It is also applied to a sort of bumblebee which victimises the busy family establishments that I have described. Although very similar in appearance the cuckoo-bumbles are placed in a distinct genus, *Psithyrus,* from *Bombus,* the ordinary bumblebees. The females of the cuckoo are stronger than those of *Bombus,* with a more powerful sting, and they lack that badge of industry and thrift, the pollen baskets on the hind legs. The female *Psithyrus* hibernates in the usual way and comes out rather late in the spring. Then, instead of founding a nest, she hunts for a nest of *Bombus* and invades it. Her entry is resisted and if it is well established and populous she may be killed. If she is successful she kills some of the workers and sometimes the queen, though there is some uncertainty about this. In any case she intimidates and subdues the legitimate inhabitants, lays her eggs in the nest and the workers bring up a brood of *Psithyrus* males and females. None of the latter of course are workers, all are reproductive females destined for renewed acts of piracy if they survive until the next summer. There are several species of *Psithyrus* each attached to one or a few host species. Cuckoo-wasps with closely similar habits afflict the lives of the social wasps, both *Polistes* and *Vespula.*

THE HONEYBEE

It has been said that the honeybee is the only insect that we know anything about. The fact is that there is a good deal more to know than about most insects, because it is an advanced species with complicated behaviour, and indeed a vast amount of research has been done on honeybees and weighty books written about them. With so much information readily available I shall make no attempt to cover the subject of the honeybee more completely than that of the other social Hymenoptera.

Its name is *Apis mellifera*; men were probably raiding its nests in the Old Stone Age and may have begun domestication of it before stone tools were replaced by copper and bronze. The three castes are much more different from each other than those of wasps or bumblebees. The males or drones are larger than the workers and have very big eyes that cover most of the head. They are unable to gather pollen and their tongues are too short to obtain nectar from flowers, though they can and do feed themselves from the honey cells, and they produce no wax. They leave the hive on warm days and sit about on flowers and leaves. The queen is also specialized for reproduction and degenerate in other respects; she also is unable to produce wax or gather nectar and pollen. She is larger and distinctly longer than the workers and has enormously developed ovaries. The workers are normal bees with pollen-baskets on their hind legs and fully equipped for gathering nectar and making honey.

The colonies are established in the wild in some dark cavity, usually a hollow tree, so they adapt well to a skep or hive. They are perennial even in temperate climates because the bees are able to store enough honey to keep a population of workers and a queen alive through the winter. Honey is stored in wax combs of hexagonal cells, and the young are brought up in cells of the same kind, just as in the social wasps. The bees and wasps each have a long history behind them of wholly separate evolution, and it is remarkable that the social species of both, using quite dissimilar materials, have developed this precise and complicated way of accommodating their larvae. Besides collecting nectar and pollen the worker bees gather resin from trees to make a substance called propolis. This is used to seal up crevices in the hive and to cover up intrusive objects which are too large to be removed. The population of workers in a strong hive may reach a maximum of 50,000 to 80,000.

During summer queens and drones are produced, and when a virgin queen flies out she is pursued by a number of drones from her own or other colonies. Several of them mate with her in succession. The drones are killed by the act of mating and the young queen returns to her hive furnished with a large store of sperm. Queens are produced under two conditions: when the colony is preparing either for swarming or for supersedure. If the former is the case the old queen flies out accompanied by a large number of workers, and a new colony is founded. Left behind in the hive are several queens still in their cells, and usually the first of these to emerge and go out on her marriage flight becomes the new queen, and she makes sure of her position by killing any other young queens which may emerge, or even before they do so. Supersedance is the process by which an old queen, whose reproductive powers are failing, is replaced by a young and vigorous one. Here, rather curiously, there is no rivalry; the new and old queens continue to live in the hive without fighting.

When queens are required the workers build special large cells and the female larvae which hatch in them are fed until they pupate on the predigested food that has come to be known as 'royal jelly', the worker larvae get this diet only for their first two days. The rule that the old queen, not a young one, accompanies the outgoing swarm is a feature that distinguishes the honeybee from all other species in which new colonies are founded in this way.

The honeybee has a few wild relatives. One of these, the giant honeybee *(Megapis dorsata)* lives in the tropical parts of eastern Asia and is considerably larger. It makes enormous combs attached to the underside of large branches, overhangs of rock and sometimes bridges and other buildings with overhanging surfaces. The nest is always a good height above the ground. These nests are sometimes attacked by a bird of prey, the honey buzzard, which eats the larvae and pupae and is protected in some way against the stings. The attacks drive the bees to a state of fury which they vent on anything moving in the vicinity. It is dangerous to approach a giant honeybees' nest if it is seen to have a large bird clinging to it; human lives have been lost from this hazard.

In the tropics all round the world there are small stingless social bees belonging to the Family Meliponidae. Most of them nest in hollow trees or branches, and at the entrance a tube or spout of wax is made which seems to serve as a beacon to guide the workers home. There are queens (no larger than the workers) and drones, and honey is stored in parts of the comb not used for breeding, just as in the honeybee. The larvae, however, are not fed by the workers, but each brood cell is stocked with pollen and honey, furnished with an egg by the queen and then sealed up, a routine recalling that seen among the solitary bees. These stingless bees have been domesticated in the New World tropics for a long period. When Columbus landed in Cuba, one of his earliest landfalls, he was given honey to eat. This must have been the product of Beechey's bee *(Melipona beecheii)* which is still kept in hollow logs by the country people of Central America.

ANTS

Ants are similar in bodily structure to wasps but can be distinguished by a feature of the stalk or waist formed by the fore-part of the abdomen just behind its junction with the thorax. All ants have one or two humps or knots on the waist, which are never present in other insects with stalked hind-bodies. Also the antennae of ants are sharply angled or elbowed. Only the reproductive males and females have wings. The workers are always wingless and the queens break off their own wings after their marriage flight. Like beetles, ants have largely abandoned wings, and the two groups share the mastery of all environments accessible to pedestrian insects. There are no solitary ants; all of them are social insects, and they have a much longer evolutionary history of social life than the wasps or bees have. The way in which they construct their nests and conduct their communal lives is so diverse, and has so many complexities and curiosities, that I can offer little more than a glimpse of them.

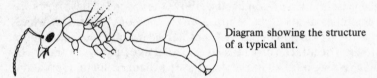

Diagram showing the structure of a typical ant.

Their nesting habits differ profoundly from those of wasps and bees. The nests normally consist of an apparently unplanned and disorderly system of chambers and galleries in which the eggs, larvae and pupae are carried about and disposed in heaps. The workers move them from one chamber to another as temperature and humidity in the nest vary in response to conditions outside. The most frequent type of nest is underground, often with a mound of soil or litter fragments thrown up above it to act as a thatch and insulator against heat and cold. Other nests are made under logs or stones, in hollow logs or trees or in hollow plant stems. In the tropics a variety of plants develop special hollow structures to accommodate ants. Some kinds make 'carton' nests by carrying soil and debris up trees and making large rounded structures among the branches by cementing the material with saliva. The most curious nests are those of the Old World tropical genus *Oecophylla* or weaving ants. These inhabit the foliage of trees and bushes and make nests by fastening together living leaves with silk. The ants themselves have no silk-producing organs, but their larvae are equipped to spin cocoons, as many ant larvae do. When construction or repair of the nest is in prospect the workers take larvae in their jaws and pass them to and fro between the leaf edges to be joined, squeezing or stimulating them in some way to produce silk as they do so. Other workers hold the leaves in position. The silk is used only in this way; the larvae do not make cocoons.

The most primitive ant societies are those of the Ponerinae, a widespread subfamily of which two species are found in Britain and a number in North America. These ants are hunters, equipped with stings and living in small communities of a few hundred. The queens are hardly distinguishable from the workers and they continue to go out and forage after the nest is established. The larvae are quite active and are fed on pieces of dismembered insects put down among them by the queen and workers. Mouth to mouth feeding of the larvae, and of the ants by each other, is not practised by the Ponerines, though it is universal and of great importance among the higher ants. The bulldog ants *(Myrmecia)* of Australia are also very primitive and have a similar economy. Both these and the Ponerines can be regarded as relics of an early worldwide population of ants that existed in the later part of the Mesozoic era.

Less primitive but still purely hunting ants are the Dorylinae, found in the tropics of Asia, Africa and America. They are most numerous and highly developed in the last two continents, where they are known as driver ants and army ants. They have no fixed home but are nomadic, operating from temporary bivouacs and continually moving on. When the queen is engaged in laying eggs they camp for about three weeks in a hollow log, but at other times they stay underneath logs for a day or two at a time, raiding out from these temporary stopping places and destroying enormous numbers of other insects. The most abundant South American genus is *Eciton,* and a queen of these ants may live from four to five years during which time she produces upwards of four million offspring.

The way of life of the higher ants can be considered by reference to their feeding habits. The majority of them have a mixed economy, hunting insects for protein needed by their growing larvae and using sugar as a source of energy. As the protein is usually predigested before being passed on to the growing generation, the ants themselves must absorb some of it; worker ants tend to live longer than those of bees and wasps. Their source of sugar is predominantly the honeydew of aphids, taken directly from the aphids rather as we take milk from cows. They associate in a similar way, but on a smaller scale, with the larvae of the Lycaenid butterflies.

The abundant species known as the garden black ant *(Lasius niger)* is a good example of the omnivorous type of ant. The nest is a large diffuse system of tunnels and chambers underground and the workers constantly seek out aphids on plants and 'milk' them, that is they persuade them to excrete a drop of sugar-water by stroking with their antennae. They also keep some kinds of aphids underground in their nests, pasturing them on roots. Even more extraordinary is their practice of collecting the eggs of the bean aphid in the autumn, keeping them in the nest and then putting them out in the spring on suitable food plants. This is the ant which sometimes invades kitchens and larders and produces enormous swarms of winged males and females in the summer.

The largest British ant is the wood ant *(Formica rufa)* whose nests appear above ground as large mounds of small dry sticks, stems and pine needles. This is really only the roof, the nest itself being in the soil underneath. The nests are often found in groups and are in communication with each other, the group forming one huge community within which there is none of the rivalry and hostility usual between separate nests of the same species. Each nest contains a number of queens and may persist almost indefinitely in the same spot, certainly for a period equivalent to a

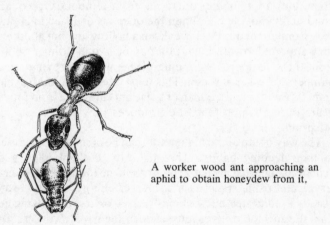

A worker wood ant approaching an aphid to obtain honeydew from it.

human lifetime. The queens are long-lived; one has been kept in captivity for 15 years. Wood ants destroy enormous numbers of woodland insects, including caterpillars injurious to forestry, but they also invade trees to use as aphid farms. Very few insects other than ants and aphids can exist on such trees, so that the aphids' enemies are excluded as well as insect defoliators. How this balance affects the welfare of the tree is not easy to determine.

Harvesting ants are an example of a group with a specialized diet. It was to them that King Solomon directed the attention of the sluggard, and they are found in rather dry regions, especially around the Mediterranean. They live on seeds, mostly of grasses, and store them underground. The seeds are brought to the nest enclosed in the chaff and this is later thrown out, so that the nest entrance is surrounded by a ring of grass-seed husks which makes it conspicuous. If the seeds in the nest get damp, due to a rainstorm, the ants bring them up and spread them out to dry, so that they do not germinate. Sometimes they do germinate and are thrown out on to the rubbish heap with the chaff and they grow there. This has given rise to the myth that they deliberately plant crops round their home, and to the name 'harvesting ant'. In many of them the workers are of various sizes, including ones with enormous heads and jaws; it is thought that these act as seed crushers, making the food available for the smaller ants which collect the seeds.

We come now to a sort of ants which do practise agriculture. These are the leaf-cutter ants, of which *Atta* is the best known genus. All of them inhabit America, from Texas south to Patagonia, and they are most numerous in the tropics. They make enormous underground nests, up to ten metres across, covered with irregular mounds of earth and harbouring certainly half-a-million ants and possibly far more. The workers go out and cut pieces out of leaves and bring them back to the nest, each one with its piece of leaf looking as if it was carrying a green flag. Inside the nest the leaves are chewed up to form compost and a certain kind of fungus is grown on it. Tiny workers act as gardeners, preventing any other sort of fungus or bacterial growth, and the fungus produces little pale coloured knobs looking rather like minute cauliflower heads. The ants and larvae feed on these and take no other food. When a queen *Atta* flies away to found a new colony she carries in a specially developed pouch under her head a small quantity of living fungus to start a culture in her nest.

An interesting and pleasant feature in the life of *Atta* ants was discovered quite recently. When they are foraging the large leaf-collecting workers are liable to attack by a parasitic fly which lays eggs on their heads; successful oviposition means certain death for the worker as the larva will feed on her brain. She can protect herself with her jaws except when she is carrying a piece of leaf. Many of the home-coming workers have, riding on their leaf, one of the tiny gardener workers; on the approach of a fly the small bodyguard rushes to intercept it with snapping jaws, and is almost always successful in repelling the enemy.

Complex inter-relations exist between different species of ants, including various sorts of parasitism. The tiny thief ant *(Solenopsis fugax)* lives in the nests of larger species in much the same way as mice inhabit our houses. It makes such narrow passages in the walls of the nest that the host species cannot pursue it, and lives by furtively stealing food that is brought in by the larger workers. A North African ant is well named *Bothriomyrmex decapitans*. The queen allows herself to be dragged by workers of another larger species into their nest. Once inside she takes refuge on the body of their queen, who is much larger than herself, and then bites off her head. After this she is adopted as the new queen and her brood is reared by the deluded workers.

'Slave-making' is another extraordinary activity. The robber ant *(Formica sanguinea)* is nearly as large as the wood ant but brighter red with the hind body grey. It lives on heaths and in wood clearings and its nest is underground with no mound to mark its position. The workers invade the nests of other ants, especially those of the black species *Formica fusca*, and carry off worker pupae to their own nest. When the black ants emerge they work as slaves in the *sanguinea* nest. The attacks appear to be well organized with scouts sent out to find weakly defended places. This practice probably has its origin in raids on other species' nests to take larvae and pupae as food; the accidental hatching of some victims in the robbers' nests could lead, in the course of evolution, to habitual raiding for slaves instead of for immediate meals. Robber ants can run their nests without slaves, but the amazon ants *(Polyergus)* cannot exist without them, and their sickle jaws are so highly adapted for fighting that they cannot look after their own young or even feed themselves. Amazon ants are found in Europe and North America but not in Britain.

TERMITES

Like ants all termites are social insects; like ants they are small and live in large or very large colonies housed in below- and above-ground systems of galleries and chambers, and like ants their communities are divided into castes including temporarily winged males and females and wingless workers and soldiers. All this has inevitably led to a superficial resemblance between the two and even to confusion and the widespread use of the misleading term 'white ants' to describe termites. This is really a case of the convergent evolution of two groups of insects whose degree of relationship with each other can be compared with that of bees to cockroaches.

Termites are placed in an Order of their own, the Isoptera, absent from Britain and mainly tropical and subtropical in distribution. They differ from the Hymenoptera in two very basic ways. They are Exopterygote insects which grow up without any larva or pupa stages, and their mode of sex determination is the normal one for animals, which tends to produce males and females in equal numbers. Their populations consist accordingly of numerous individuals of both sexes varying in size from hatchlings, which are just very small but active termites, to fully grown individuals. Normally all of these except the 'king' and 'queen' are sterile and wingless, the majority workers of various sizes and ages, with a minority of 'soldiers', specialized for defence and incapable even of feeding themselves.

In the European *Kalotermes flavicollis*, one of the few well studied species, there about nine instars and wing-buds appear after the seventh. A young termite that reaches the seventh instar may remain indefinitely without moulting again, and these individuals are called 'false workers' because they are the nearest thing that *Kalotermes* has to a worker caste. Alternatively the seventh-instar insect may develop into a soldier, acquiring the large head and jaws which make it a specialized fighter; or it may continue development, growing wing-buds and eventually the wings of a male or female reproductive of the kind which flies away when a swarm leaves the nest. Finally, the termites that develop wing-buds may stop short of growing wings, which remain rudimentary, and turn into 'supplementary reproductives', that is males and females capable of mating and laying fertile eggs, but destined to stay in the nest. These develop in the population if the

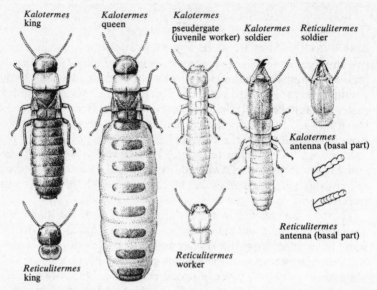

Kalotermes
king

Kalotermes
queen

Kalotermes
pseudergate
(juvenile worker)

Kalotermes
soldier

Reticulitermes
soldier

Kalotermes
antenna (basal part)

Reticulitermes
antenna (basal part)

Reticulitermes
worker

Reticulitermes
king

Caste differences in *Kalotermes* and the other European termite genus, *Reticulitermes*. (From M. C. Chinery *A Field Guide to the Insects of Britain and Northern Europe*, Collins.)

king and queen are removed or meet with an accident. In the true worker caste of the higher termites the insect assumes a definite form beyond which it cannot develop by further moulting.

By this sort of differentiation an artificial colony of 20 to 30 identical third instar young *Kalotermes* can produce a colony in which all castes are represented. This is a very different sort of organization from that in an ants' nest (or those of social wasps and bees) in which all, except the few winged males, are females of one kind or another, their development into worker, soldier or queen being determined by the food they get as larvae.

It is generally supposed that caste is determined in the termites by hormones that are secreted by each caste and inhibit development into that caste. They are distributed through the population by mouth-to-mouth feeding and by the recycling of incompletely digested excrement. Thus supplementary reproductives only develop in the absence of the king and queen, and soldiers are only produced if casualties reduce the percentage of them below the level normally maintained, thus reducing the average intake of soldier hormone by young termites.

I have mentioned king and queen termites. This is another feature in which the Isoptera differ from the social Hymenoptera. The queen does not have a single mating flight and live thenceforth as an extremely prolific widow. A king and queen termite live permanently together in the nest, mating at intervals and fed and tended by the workers. In the more primitive termites, including *Kalotermes*, the king and queen live in the more central parts of an ill-defined colony excavated in wood, but in the more advanced types a 'royal chamber' is made in which the two live together, the queen being so enlarged as to be quite immobile.

In swarming and nest founding termites behave very much as ants do. Large numbers of winged males and females issue from the nest, fly a little way and then drop to the ground and break off their wings. Both sexes do this, after which they meet on the ground and together search for a place where they can dig a tunnel and make a small chamber. Mating then takes place and a small initial brood of workers is produced. Flights of winged termites are occasions for feasting by all the insectivorous inhabitants of the area, and only a minute proportion ever meet a partner and found a new colony, and numerous hazards eliminate all but very few of the colonies that are founded.

Nests are of various types. The more primitive and simply organized Families burrow in wood. Those of the advanced Family Termitidae may be underground, or partly so and partly in mounds or special above-ground structures called termitaria, or more rarely carton nests in trees.

The so-called dry-wood termites, which include *Kalotermes*, burrow in wood, feeding on it as they burrow, and their nests have no definite form or fixed boundaries. These are the termites whose useful function in nature is to consume fallen timber in forests and return its substance to the soil. They are naturally unable to distinguish between the wood of a fallen tree and the structural timber of a building, and in tropical countries they are responsible for serious damage to fence-posts, houses and wooden containers of all kinds. Neglected books, being made of wood pulp, may be rapidly destroyed. These termites never venture into the open and so their presence can go wholly undetected until books or packing cases are inspected or the timber of the house is so honeycombed that it collapses. They defeat such measures as concrete supports for the timber of houses by building covered passages made of chewed-up wood or soil, which are slowly advanced over any surface to be explored in search of dry dead wood. There are some Families which nest in damp wood, with the nest extending into the ground, and timber in contact with the ground may be damaged by them.

The nests of the most advanced Family, the Termitidae, include the most spectacular structures made by any insects. Many of them nest underground and build enormous towers or steeples over their nests reaching a height of five or six metres and a circumference at the base of 15 metres or more. The inside of these termitaria is divided into numerous chambers and galleries and the thick outer wall is made of a sort of cement of saliva or excrement and clay, and is extremely hard. In Africa these termitaria are serious obstacles when ground is being cleared and levelled. The largest resist even modern earth-moving machinery and have to be shattered with explosives.

Nothern Australia is the home of the well known compass termite which builds termitaria up to four metres high, each one shaped like a wedge standing on its base and having its long axis always precisely north and south. It is thought that this serves to minimize rapid changes in temperature inside the nest. In the morning the sun will shine directly on the east side of the nest; as it rises higher and increases in strength its rays strike more and more obliquely until noon, when neither side receives direct illumination. In the afternoon and evening the sequence is repeated in reverse. In cool weather the termites crowd to the side that is receiving the sun's heat and on hot days they go to the shaded side.

The big termitaria may persist for many years. In 1872 the top of a steeple-like nest in Australia was knocked off to allow a telegraph wire to pass over it, and it was still flourishing in 1935. It must have existed for a long time before 1872 to have reached such a height.

It is in the large nests of the Termitidae that the enormous sausage-like queen termites are found. After the foundation of a successful colony the abdomen of the queen expands to accommodate more and more eggs. The sclerites or segmental plates of the abdomen keep their normal size and appear as brown islands on the pale coloured body, most of whose surface is formed by the greatly expanded intersegmental membrane. The abdomen of a queen termite may weigh 1,500 times as much as the rest of her body. A queen of one of the African tower-builders has been seen to lay 36,000 eggs in 24 hours, but it is not known whether this performance continues throughout the year. No attempt has been made to count the inhabitants of one of these huge termitaria, but they must certainly number several and perhaps many millions. Queen termites are believed to live as long as fifty years, but really very little is known about this aspect of their lives.

Some genera of the Termitidae are distinguished by having soldiers of a peculiar kind called nasutes. Instead of being equipped with powerful jaws they have the front of the head drawn out to form a spout through which a sticky liquid can be ejected. This is very effective against ants, which are the most serious enemies that termites have to contend with.

All termites are primarily vegetarian. Those of the wood-boring Families subsist on wood and are enabled to digest it by the presence of a variety of the micro-organisms called protozoa in their intestine. These have the power to break down the cellulose to sugars and other substances, a thing that no insects or higher animals can do unaided. These particular Protozoa can live in no habitat other than an insect intestine, and the only other insect in which they are found is a North American wood-feeding cockroach.

The higher termites seek food outside their nests, always vegetable matter, sometimes living, more often dead and decaying. The builders of the big termitaria store chewed up vegetable matter underground, and fungus grows on it on which the termites feed, a remarkable parallel with the *Atta* ants. If the social Hymenoptera can teach mankind lessons in industry and population control, we have another important one to learn from termites: that of recycling to avoid waste. The workers of the South African black mound termite *(Amitermes hastatus)* studied by Dr S. H. Skaife eat decayed wood and reed stems. Cast skins inside the nest are also eaten and any termites that die. The excrement is eaten by the workers over and over again until it has the form of a sticky black paste containing no nourishment whatever. Even this is not wasted, but is used to cement together sand grains in building the hard walls of the nest. Life in a black mound termites' nest must be a little like that in a science fiction writer's interstellar space ship, but I doubt if any writer's imagination has taken him as far as the reality that is normal life inside one of hard black nests of *Amitermes hastatus*.

CHAPTER 4

A CATALOGUE OF INSECTS

CLASSIFICATION AND TAXONOMY EXPLAINED

It is impossible to discuss insects at the level aimed at in this book without frequent reference to their classification. The largest divisions of the Animal Kingdom are the phyla, and our first chapter starts by defining insects as a Class, the Insecta, within the phylum Arthropoda. The next two major groups are Order (a subdivision of Class) and Family (a subdivision of Order), followed by the genus and species that comprise the Latin or binomial name, which is always printed in italics with an initial capital for the genus but never for the species. I have used initial capitals for Class, Order and Family as a reminder that the words are being used in a special sense as part of the vocabulary of taxonomy. This system of classifying and naming, now greatly elaborated, was invented in the mid-18th century by the Swedish naturalist Carl von Linné, himself more generally known by his latinized name Carolus Linnaeus.

Thus the common swallowtail butterfly of Europe and temperate Asia, besides being first an arthropod and secondly an insect, belongs to the Order Lepidoptera or butterflies and moths, the Family Papilionidae, the genus *Papilio* and the species *machaon*. It was named *Papilio machaon* by Linnaeus, 'papilio' being the Latin for a butterfly and Machaon the name of a Greek physician who took part in the Trojan war. The early zoologists were all classical scholars and the gods, goddesses and heroes of antiquity feature largely in early taxonomy. Other species, such as the American tiger swallowtail *(P. glaucus)* and the African mocker swallowtail *(P. dardanus)* are included in the genus *Papilio*. '*Papilio machaon*' may seem rather a mouthful, but it serves to identify the butterfly all over the world, regardless of the language used in this country or that. Without some provision of this kind entomologists of different nations could not exchange ideas about insects intelligibly.

Insects are so numerous that intermediate categories have to be used in addition to the primary ones, from phylum to species, that I have indicated. Usually they are self-explanatory: subclass comes between Class and Order, superfamily and subfamily above and below Family. Less explicit terms such as 'division' and 'section' are also used. Local isolated populations of a species may become sufficiently differentiated to be recognizable, and are indicated by subspecific names. The British subspecies of the swallowtail butterfly is called *Papilio machaon britannicus*. It can be distinguished at sight from the French *P. machaon gorganus*, the Alaskan *P. machaon aliaska* and the Scandinavian *P. machaon machaon*. The last named is the butterfly originally described by Linnaeus and his name *machaon* is repeated to designate the subspecies.

Species and subspecies are realities, indicating populations of animals which remain separate by breeding only among themselves. As a general rule separate species cannot interbreed and produce offspring that can continue breeding. Separate subspecies can do so if brought together artificially. If their progeny fail to breed successfully this may be regarded as grounds for giving them the status of species.

The higher categories, from phylum to genus, are purely artificial and created to indicate progressively closer degrees of similarity and relationship, and their boundaries are often a matter of dispute among taxonomists. The fact, however, that animals can be readily classified in a heirarchy, as such a system of progressively inclusive categories is called, is a clear indication that they are truly related to one another, and is one of the most powerful arguments for the reality of evolution.

The purpose of taxonomy, the science of classifying and naming living things, is really two-fold. In practice it provides a system for biologists by means of which they can indicate precisely what kind of animal or plant they are writing or talking about. But taxonomists always endeavour to make their nomenclature reflect the evolutionary history of the creatures to which they give names. As we shall see, convenience and evolutionary realism sometimes have to be balanced against each other to arrive at an acceptable system.

When describing growth and metamorphosis of insects in Chapter 2, I referred to the three divisions Apterygota, Exopterygota and Endopterygota. These are not, in fact, of equal rank. The primarily wingless insects form a subclass, the Apterygota, and all the winged or secondarily wingless ones another subclass, the Pterygota. These fall into two divisions, the Exopterygota and

Endopterygota, according to the sort of metamorphosis they undergo during growth. The terms Hemimetabola and Holometabola are also used as equivalents of Exopterygota and Endopterygota. They imply that the two groups are respectively half-hearted and whole-hearted in their metamorphosis.

This is the traditional primary classification within which the insects are divided into Orders. In recent years, however, two of the Exopterygote Orders, the Ephemeroptera (mayflies) and Odonata (dragonflies) have been separated from all the rest of the Pterygote insects to form a division called the Palaeoptera or 'ancient wings' and the remaining Pterygote Orders classed together as the Neoptera or 'new-style wings'. It seems probable that this classification, based on the wing venation, reflects a more fundamental evolutionary divergence of the winged insects than that indicated by their type of metamorphosis. Both provide a realistic approach to insect classification and they can be regarded as complementary to each other.

In reading the following 'catalogue' it should be borne in mind that the subclass Apterygota is really a category of convenience comprising four Orders of small primitive arthropods related to the higher insects in widely varying degrees and not closely related to each other. All, however, are wingless and have no history of wings in their ancestry. The two figures given after each Order represent respectively the total number of species that have been described and the number known to be natives of Britain. The first figures, especially, are often little more than guesses and authorities often disagree about them. In three recent text books of entomology, with publication dates ranging over about ten years, the world figures for Lepidoptera are respectively 100,000, 140,000 and 200,000. I have compromised at 150,000. Nevertheless the figures give some idea of the numbers of insects known to us.

INSECT SUBCLASSES AND ORDERS

APTERYGOTA

1. Thysanura (350; 23). Commonly called bristletails, the most familiar members of this Order are two species that have become domesticated, the silverfish *(Lepisma saccharina)* and the firebrat *(Thermobia domestica)*. The former is common in kitchens and the latter likes even warmer surroundings, especially bakehouses.

PLATE 17. *Nemoptera sinuata* (Order Neuroptera) photographed in Turkey.

PLATE 18. *Above*, a brown lacewing, *Hemerobius lutescens*; *below*, a darter dragonfly, *Sympetrum striolatum*.

Another bristletail that is quite often seen is *Petrobius maritimus*, which runs and jumps about among rocks close to the edge of the sea. In countries with a warm and fairly dry climate various kinds can be found by turning over stones and some species live as guests or commensals in ants' nests.

The silverfish, a typical member of the primitive Order, Thysanura.

Bristletails are small insects with smooth tapered bodies covered with scales rather like those on a butterfly's wing. They have long antennae and three long tail feelers behind. Their mouthparts have the same design as those of a cockroach, and of all the Apterygota they are the closest relatives of the higher insects. A feature of interest is the presence of rudimentary appendages on the under segments of the abdomen, probably vestiges of the limbs of some centipede-like ancestor. Also the wings of the higher insects are foreshadowed by lobes called paranota on the thorax of some Thysanura. This feature and the reproduction and growth of the silverfish have been described in an earlier chapter.

2. Diplura (400; 11). Under bark and in leaf-mould and compost one sometimes sees a tiny insect looking like a piece of white thread with a pair of even finer threads projecting from head and tail. Although it has no eyes it hates the light and always scuttles for shelter when it is exposed. This is *Campodea,* a typical member of this Order. The Diplura used to be included with the Thysanoptera, but the antennae of *Campodea* and its relatives have numerous segments provided with minute muscles, a peculiar feature that links them with the centipedes. They have only two feeler-like appendages on the tail and differ from bristletails also in the fact that the mouthparts are enclosed in a deep pouch. The largest Diplura are species of the genus *Japyx* which reach 5 cm. in length and have pincers on the tail like an earwig. They are found in Australia.

3. Protura (50; 17). These are very small white insects, 1 to 2 mm long, that live in similar situations to the Diplura. They have no antennae, but hold up their front legs when they move and evidently use them as tactile organs. They have 8 abdominal segments when they hatch from the egg and add three more later, a mode of growth found in no other insects, and their relationships are quite obscure.

4. Collembola (1,500; 260). The springtails are all very small insects that exist in enormous numbers on and below the soil and among herbage, and some of them live on the surface of the water. One species, *Anurida maritima,* is a truly marine insect that floats on the surface film in rock pools; at high tide it enters rock crevices and is submerged. Their English name derives from a peculiar jumping organ, a fork-shaped appendage attached to the hind end of the abdomen and folded forwards. It is held in place by a catch, and the insect jumps by applying tension to the fork and then suddenly releasing it from the catch. A springtail jumps rather like a mousetrap that is set and then dropped upside-down. The apparatus is lacking in springtails that live permanently under the soil. They have another peculiar organ, the ventral tube, which is sucker-like and projects downwards from the front end of the abdomen. It was once thought to be an adhesive organ used in climbing, and the name Collembola means 'glue-peg'. Its real function is probably to absorb moisture.

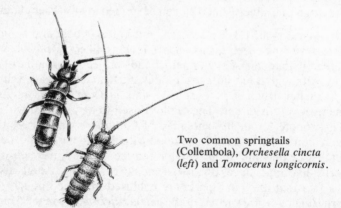

Two common springtails (Collembola), *Orchesella cincta* (*left*) and *Tomocerus longicornis.*

The abdomen of all other insects, including the other Apterygota, has eleven segments, that of Collembola only six; and there are other un-insect-like features in their anatomy and embryology. The fact is that the Collembola have been classified with the insects because they are six-legged land arthropods. They are not on the 'family tree' of the true insects or anywhere near it, and in a strictly natural classification they would be placed in a Class of their own. There is another remarkable piece of evidence of their separateness: by a happy freak of preservation wonderfully perfect fossils have been found in Scotland in a flint-like rock which is of Devonian age in the geological record. These include primitive land plants and also quite recognizable springtails, not very different from those of today. This indicates that the Collembola have existed as a distinct group of animals for something like 400 million years.

PTERYGOTA: Exopterygota (Hemimetabola)

5. Ephemeroptera (1,000; 46). Mayflies are well known mainly because anglers for trout are guided by their mass emergences and tie their artificial flies to simulate them. They are soft-bodied insects with feeble flight and very short imaginal life, some of them less than a day. They have large eyes and minute antennae and never feed as imagines. After they leave the water and acquire their wings the stomach and intestine are inflated with air to give the insect added buoyancy in flight. There are usually three, sometimes two, long jointed appendages at the tip of the abdomen, recalling those of the silverfish, and the venation of the wings is very like that of fossil wings of Palaeodictyoptera, the most ancient of all winged insects. The hind-wings are always relatively small and may be absent.

Mayflies are unique among insects in undergoing an ecdysis after the wings are developed. The nymph crawls out of the water, or floats to the surface, and the insect that emerges expands its wings. In this stage it is dull coloured and has feeble powers of flight; this is the 'dun' of anglers. It settles again and sheds a very thin pellicle from its body, limbs and wings, after which the wings are bright and shining and the body fully coloured. When at rest mayflies always hold their wings together over their backs, like a butterfly. After a brief flight they mate, lay their eggs in the water and die.

The early stages are always aquatic. The nymphs of various species are adapted for life in flowing or still waters, or for burrowing in mud. The first are flattened and have hooked spines for clinging to rocks. The burrowers have cylindrical bodies and legs adapted for digging. All of them breathe by a series of gills on each side of the body. They feed on algae and other vegetable matter and have long lives, some species as much as three years. We are accustomed to think of insects in terms of the imago and look upon the early stages as representing a sort of infancy and childhood. It is more realistic to regard mayflies as long-lived aquatic insects, with their winged life a brief reproductive episode that occupies perhaps a thousandth of the period of their existence.

6. Odonata (5,000; 43). The dragonflies and mayflies both have a long history in the fossil record and are the only living representatives of the Palaeoptera or 'ancient-winged' insects. In other respects they could hardly be more different. Mayflies are vegetarians during their long period of growth and as imagines are feeble fliers and abstain from food altogether. Dragonflies have powerful flight and are fierce predators throughout their lives. All of them are large, as insects go, and some are among the largest flying insects. They have minute antennae and depend for their appreciation of their surroundings on their enormous and very efficient eyes. They use their legs for seizing prey rather than walking, and all have the strange method of mating that I described in Chapter 2. The wings have a number of longitudinal veins joined by innumerable short cross-veins, forming a network that is quite unlike the venation of any other insect. Towards the tip of the leading edge of each wing there is a quadrangular pigmented mark called the pterostigma. The wings are usually clear but may be wholly or partly pigmented, and when they are so this feature often differs in the two sexes.

For convenience I have used the name dragonfly as equivalent to the whole Order, but it is often confined to one of the two main suborders, the Anisoptera. The other suborder, the Zygoptera, are the much more slender and lightly built damselflies. These also differ in having the fore- and hind-wings closely similar, and in resting with the wings held together over the back. In the Anisoptera (which means 'unequal wings') the hind-wings are broadened at the base, and at rest both pairs are extended on each side. Two rare species from Asia comprise the living members of a third

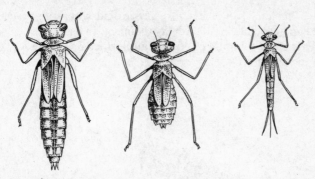

Three types of dragonfly nymphs: *left to right*, *Brachytron pratense*; *Sympetrum* sp.; *Coenagrion pulchellum*. The first two are Anisoptera, the last a damselfly (Zygoptera).

suborder (well represented as fossils) that is intermediate between the two.

The aquatic nymphs are predators on water animals, mainly other insects, but those of the big hawker dragonflies may take small fish. The two suborders have gills of a very different form. Zygoptera nymphs have three delicate leaf-like gills at the hind end of the body. In those of the Anisoptera the gills line the wall of the hind gut or rectum and water for respiration is drawn in and out. It can be shot out with such force that the insect is propelled forwards. This habit of combining breathing and jet propulsion is shared with the marine squids and cuttlefish.

Dragonflies are a very remarkable group of animals. They are numerous and successful, but by evolutionary standards they are quite out of date. They have an immensely long geological history; their immediate ancestors the gigantic Protodonata or dawn-dragonflies of the Carboniferous period were already evolved 300 million years ago, and true dragonflies were the dominant predatory insects both before and during the 100-million-year reign of the dinosaurs. In their structure they display archaic features, especially in the venation and musculature of the wings. In spite of this their speed and agility in flight excels that of most 'modern' insects.

7. **Dictyoptera** (5,300; 3). Cockroaches and praying mantids seem unlikely candidates for inclusion in the same Order, but they share similarities in structure, especially of the wings, the fore-wings being thickened and leathery in both suborders, but still used in

flight. The hind-wings are very broad and when not in use are folded up like a fan. Also both lay their eggs in batches enclosed in an egg-capsule or ootheca. Some authorities do, however, place them in separate Orders.

Common cockroach, male (*left*), female and an ootheca.

The cockroaches (suborder Blattaria) are mainly tropical and subtropical in distribution, but are well known because some subtropical species have become household pests in all parts of the world. The large so-called American cockroach (*Periplaneta americana*), which is really North African in origin, breeds in captivity as happily as it does in unhygienic kitchen premises, and is used as an introduction to insects for students, who dissect it and mount its mouthparts on microscope slides. the choice is a good one because one could not have a more generalized insect type. Cockroaches, indeed, are among the most ancient insects known, although they are classed with the Neoptera. Fossils of them, very like the modern forms, are found in the coal measures of the Carboniferous period, and at that time, 300 million years ago, they were so diverse and widespread that they must have been in existence already for many millions of years.

Cockroaches are in most respects unspecialized. This applies both to their anatomy and also to their way of life, which is to keep out of harm's way and eat virtually anything from which nourishment can be extracted. But in their way of producing their eggs they are curiously specialized. The eggs are deposited in a neatly compartmented sclerotized capsule called an ootheca, which is developed internally as the eggs are laid. The common cockroach (*Blatta orientalis*) carries it about, partly extruded, for a time and then cements it into a crevice and leaves it. She can produce up to nine capsules each containing 16 eggs. The German cockroach

(*Blattella germanica*, also from Africa) carries her ootheca about for weeks and drops it only when the eggs are about to hatch.

The mantids (suborder Mantodea) are highly specialized predators and will only eat prey that they have captured alive, usually another insect. The prothorax is greatly elongated, the fore-legs are spined and adapted for seizing prey and the eyes are large. If these features are removed, what remains is not unlike a cockroach. Mantids hunt by lying in wait, usually well camouflaged, and the attitude in which they hold their fore-legs has led to the epithet 'praying' that is often applied to them; 'preying' would be more realistic. The female mantis lays eggs in an ootheca which is extruded as a frothy secretion that hardens to a spongy texture. The mantids are mainly tropical, a few extending to warm temperate regions such as those of the United States and southern Europe. None are found in Britain.

8. Isoptera (1700; 0). The elaborate social economy of termites or 'white ants' is described in Chapter 3. In their affinities they are, of course, not remotely related to ants, but are really highly evolved social cockroaches. In most termites this relationship is far from obvious, especially as the wings, when they are present, are very different. In almost all termites the fore- and hind-wings are similar, wholly membranous and the latter lack any basal lobe. This feature is present in cockroaches, and they also have the fore-wings thickened and leathery.

Fortunately a very primitive type of termite has survived in Australia. This is *Mastotermes darwiniensis*, and it is wide-spread and often abundant in the tropical north of the continent. It attacks structural timber, eats stored products including paper, flour and hay and is sometimes a pest of sugar cane; some Australian people might regard the opening word of this paragraph as inappropriate. Its continued existence is nevertheless fortunate for entomologists, as it has primitive and unmistakably cockroach-like features. The reproductive individuals are unusually large and their hind-wings have a well developed lobe on the hind margin. The egg-laying organ or ovipositor of the female is of cockroach type and the eggs are laid in a capsular structure, arranged in two rows of 12 eggs in each. Fossil relatives of *Mastotermes* are known from the Eocene epoch, 50 to 60 million years ago. Primitive termites certainly existed long before that, but fossils of them have yet to be found.

9. Embioptera (140; 0). A small Order of small insects found in warm countries and forming an evolutionary side-line. Their nearest relatives seem to be the termites, and it is a point of interest that they show rudiments of social behaviour. They live under stones and bark in irregular chambers made of silken threads which they spin from glands in the tarsi of the fore-legs. Groups of some size live together including developing young as well as males and females, but there is no exchange of food between individuals. Only the males are winged; the females never develop any trace of wings and have no apparent metamorphosis, growing and developing in a similar way to the Apterygote insects.

10. Plecoptera (1,300; 34). Stoneflies are soft-bodied, weakly flying insects seldom found far from the water in which they pass their early stages. The head and thorax are broad, the antennae rather long and the wings are folded over each other and held flat over the insect's back. There are two jointed cerci at the hinder end. The nymphs live in flowing water and breathe by filamentous gills which grow in tufts at the base of the legs. Some are predatory, others feed on algae, and the nymphal life is long, sometimes nearly four years. Stoneflies are Neopterous analogues of the mayflies; although they are a more advanced type of insect, they also are archaic animals with a long fossil history.

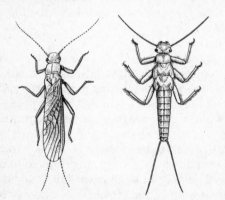

A typical stonefly (*left*) and the aquatic nymph of one of these insects. (From M. C. Chinery *A Field Guide to the Insects of Britain and Northern Europe*, Collins.)

11. Grylloblattodea (6; 0). Also known as the **Notoptera**, this is a very small Order consisting of six rare species found in cold mountainous areas of North America, Russia and Japan. They live under stones and are wingless and eyeless, and are 'living fossils',

surviving precariously from the past in an inhospitable habitat
where they avoid competition from more advanced insects. They
seem to form a link between the Dictyoptera and the Orthoptera;
the name *Grylloblatta* means 'cricket-cockroach'.

12. Dermaptera (900; 5). These are the earwigs, of which the
common earwig *(Forficula auricularia)* is a familiar insect but
other members of the Order are seldom noticed. The fore-wings
are short tegmina or covering sheaths and the hind-wings are
folded under them in an amazingly complex way. The cerci at the
tail end are transformed to form forceps. The common earwig, and
probably other species too, brood and guard their eggs and newly
hatched young. Most of them are small, but the giant earwig of St.
Helena *(Labidura herculeana)* may be 8 cm. or more in length.
Two parasitic earwigs are known, one on an African species of rat,
the other on bats in Southeast Asia.

13. Phasmida (2,000; 0). These are the stick-insects and leaf-
insects, mostly large sluggish insects of warm climates, most
numerous in the tropics of Asia. Some have leathery forewings or
tegmina, covering broad fan-shaped hind-wings, but many are
wingless. Nearly all are camouflaged for concealment among twigs
and leaves, some elaborately so. They lay curious hard seed-like
eggs which are dropped on the ground and take a long time to
hatch, and some species are known to reproduce parthenogenetically, that is without fertilization by a male.

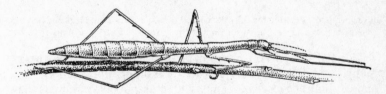

A stick insect, *Carausius morosus*.

14. Orthoptera (10,000; 30). This and the last seven Orders (from
Dictyoptera) are sometimes classed together as the Orthopteroid
insects, indicating that they form a natural group culminating in the
great Order Orthoptera, the crickets, grasshoppers and locusts.
There are two features that are characteristic of members of this
Order. Firstly most of them have the hind pair of legs greatly

enlarged for jumping, a feature that already appears in the newly hatched nymphs; an alternative name for the Order is **Saltatoria**, 'the jumpers'. Secondly the habit of singing by stridulation runs through the whole Order.

They fall into three principal groups. The bush-crickets, long-horned grasshoppers or katydids have long antennae and the females are armed with a curved, flattened rather sword-like ovipositor. The tarsi of the legs are 4-segmented. The second group, the crickets and mole-crickets, also have long antennae, but the ovipositor, when present, is straight, and the tarsi are 3-segmented. The members of both these groups stridulate by rubbing together specially modified parts of the right and left tegmina or fore-wings, and both have hearing organs in the tibia of the fore-legs. The third group comprises the grasshoppers and locusts, which have short antennae and a short ovipositor, and stridulate by rubbing the hind femur against the fore-wing. The hearing organ is at the base of the abdomen. In formal classification the first two groups are put in a sub-order, the Ensifera, and the grasshoppers in another, the Caelifera.

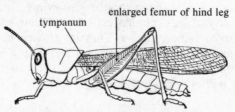

enlarged femur of hind leg

tympanum

A grasshopper, showing the fully developed wings, enlarged hind legs and hearing organs or tympana. (From A. D. Imms *Insect Natural History*, Collins.)

The question of an English name for the first group has never really been settled. 'Long-horned grasshopper' is cumbersome and wrongly suggests an affinity with grasshoppers, whereas they are obviously more nearly related to crickets. The name 'katydid' is of American origin; it refers to the song of one genus and is in no way descriptive of the whole group. Bush-cricket seems the most suitable name, or they can be called tettigoniids after the most important Family. The majority of these insects live among the foliage of trees and are coloured green, and their fore-wings are often formed and marked to resemble leaves.

Crickets are mainly ground dwellers, often making burrows, and one, the house cricket, has become domesticated. Mole crickets are rather large, strange looking insects with the hind-legs not adapted for jumping but the fore-legs modified to form powerful digging tools. They live mainly underground, but some of them can fly, and the males sit at the mouths of their burrows and sing loudly at dusk.

The grasshoppers and locusts mostly live in grass and low bushes or on the ground. They bear two conflicting images, the merry little grasshopper singing in the meadow and the swarming locust, bringer of disaster and starvation. If locusts did not congregate in huge destructive swarms they would be regarded just as big grasshoppers.

15. Zoraptera (16; 0). Perhaps the most obscure of all the insect Orders; only 16 species are known, all minute insects included in one genus, and confined to warm climates. We have finished with the Orthopteroid insects and now go on to the Hemipteroid group (the next five Orders), and the Zoraptera are in some ways intermediate between the two. They were at one time regarded as a branch of the Psocoptera.

16. Psocoptera (1,100; 70). This Order consists of minute soft-bodied insects of which certain particularly small wingless species have become domesticated and are called book-lice. These are the little creatures, often miscalled 'mites', that wreak havoc in moth and butterfly collections which are not protected by a deterrent such as naphthalene. The more typical species live out of doors, many of them on the trunks and branches of trees, feeding on lichens and fungi. If the lichen-covered twigs of an old fruit tree are shaken into a tray or inverted umbrella specimens of the genus *Mesopsocus* often appear, looking like small, round-bodied, six-legged spiders with a pattern of vertical stripes on the clypeus, a square plate that forms a 'face' between the eyes. Some Psocoptera have two pairs of delicate wings and look rather like aphids. There some also that spin silk from the labium and make net-like covers on bark under which they assemble in swarms. They are the most primitive of the Hemipteroid insects, which are now being described.

Mesopsocus sp., a rather large member of the Psocoptera that lives on bark and dead twigs.

17. Mallophaga (2,600; 260). The biting lice or bird-lice are external parasites of birds and a few of mammals. They feed mainly by chewing the feathers and scaly surface of the skin. It is possible that they are derived from nest-inhabiting Psocoptera that took to a parasitic existence. The various Orders of birds generally have particular Families of bird-lice attached to them, and it can be supposed that the hosts and parasites have evolved together during geological time. Attempts have been made to settle the taxonomic affinities of peculiar birds, such as flamingos, by reference to their lice. In this case an affinity with ducks and geese is indicated, but other lines of evidence associate flamingos with storks and herons.

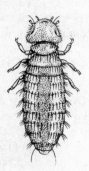 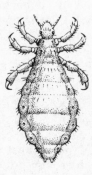

Left, a biting louse (Mallophaga) and *right*, a sucking louse (Anopleura). Most biting lice have two claws on each foot, the sucking lice have a single one. (From M. C. Chinery *A Field Guide to the Insects of Britain and Northern Europe*, Collins.)

18. Anoplura or **Siphunculata** (225; 24). There seems to be no agreement on which is the better name for the Order comprising the sucking lice. They resemble the Mallophaga, but the mouthparts are modified for piercing and are pushed out through a small sucking tube just in front of the head.

Like the Mallophaga they are all wingless parasites, and here again there seems to have been parallel evolution of parasite and host. The genus *Enderleinellus* is confined to squirrels, and distinct species of *Pediculus* infest men and chimpanzees. The *Pediculus humanus* of man has split into two biological races, one which lives in the hair of the head (race or subspecies *capitis*) and the other on the clothes in contact with the skin (race *corporis*). They are just distinguishable in appearance and must have evolved since men took to wearing clothes. The body louse is the carrier of the dangerous epidemic disease typhus.

19. Thysanoptera (2,000; 180). These are the tiny insects called thrips or thunder flies. They are like elongated lice but have narrow wings consisting of strips of chitin with a fringe of hairs on each side. They infest plants and numbers can often be seen in flowers, especially dandelions, looking like little black printer's hyphens. In hot thundery weather they fly in huge numbers and settle annoyingly on people's hands and faces.

The Thysanoptera have a peculiar type of metamorphosis. There are four or five nymphal instars, the first two being like the adult but having no sign of wings. The next two or three are resting stages to which the terms 'prepupa' and 'pupa' have been applied, the last one' before the adult being the 'pupa', and during these instars external wing-buds appear. There is an obvious resemblance to the changes undergone by the Endopterygote insects, but it probably represents a parallel rather than an evolutionary link, and thrips are best regarded as Hemipteroid insects.

20. Hemiptera (56,000; 1,400). The words 'bug', 'bugbear' and 'bogey' formerly meant a small unpleasant ghost or goblin, but 'bug' became transferred, with good reason, to the furtive and disgusting bedbug and later, quite unreasonably, to any sort of insect. Entomologists use it to indicate only the Hemiptera, of which the bedbug is a member. This is the largest and most diverse of the Exopterygote Orders and forms the culmination of the Hemipteroid insects. Although they are so diverse the bugs have one very constant feature in common, the way in which the mouthparts are adapted for piercing and sucking up liquid food. This has been described in Chapter 2. They fall into two well marked suborders, the Homoptera and Heteroptera, distinguished by the structure of the fore-wings. In the Homoptera these are usually membranous, like the hind-wings, and are of the same

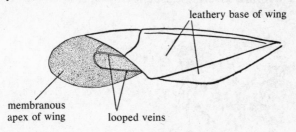

Left fore-wing of a plant bug of the family Miridae. (From A. D. Imms *Insect Natural History*, Collins.)

texture throughout. In Heteroptera the basal half to two-thirds of the fore-wing is leathery and sharply divided from the membranous tip. When at rest the fore-wings overlap flat on the back and the leathery part protects the folded hind-wings.

The Homoptera are all feeders on plant sap and discharge from the anus quantities of a clear sugary liquid, which represents the great excess of sugar over protein in their diet. This excretion is the honey-dew which is voided onto leaves in huge quantities by aphids and is relished by many kinds of ants, night-flying moths and other insects. Aphids are the most numerous and familiar Homopterous bugs. The froghoppers (Cercopidae) live as nymphs in masses of froth, which they produce by blowing bubbles in their honeydew. Under the name of 'cuckoo-spit' these froth masses are familiar and conspicuous on low herbage, and they probably serve to protect the nymphs from predators. Adult froghoppers jump like grasshoppers.

The vociferous cicadas include the largest Homoptera and the lantern-flies (Fulgoridae) are large tropical insects, strangely shaped and often brightly coloured. Early stay-at-home entomologists, when confronted with specimens of these spectacular bugs called them lantern-flies simply because they thought such remarkable insects ought to be luminous; in fact none of them is so. White-flies (Aleyrodidae) are familiar to keepers of greenhouses and cultivators of cabbages. Their white colour is due to a fine powdery wax excreted all over the body and wings. This excretion of wax is another characteristic of Homoptera and reaches its greatest development in the mealy-bugs and scale-insects (superfamily Coccoidea). They live on plants, just as aphids do, but become covered with a waxy exudation. In the female scale-insects all the cast skins or exuviae are glued together with wax to form a covering scale under which the female develops

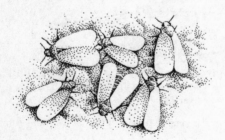

White-flies, *Aleyrodes brassicae*, crowded on a cabbage leaf.

in a degenerate form, hardly recognizable as an insect. The males are minute with only the fore-wings developed and no functional mouthparts or power of feeding. Many scale-insects are pests of cultivated trees, but the Indian species *Laccifer lacca* is the basis of shellac production. The exudation of *Trabutina mannipara*, which feeds on tamarisk in the deserts of the Middle East, falls to the ground in the form of scales and is used as food by the Bedouin people; it was in fact the 'manna' on which the wandering Israelites subsisted in the Sinai desert.

Many of the Heteroptera look rather like beetles, but their beak-like mouthparts immediately distinguish them. A number of them have successfully invaded the freshwater environment; these include the water-boatmen (Corixidae), the back-swimmers (Notonectidae) and the water scorpions (Nepidae). The first two Families swim in a similar way, by rowing with hind-legs beautifully adapted to work as oars. Corixids are vegetable feeders, Notonectids are predators, whose sharp beak can inflict a painful 'sting' if they are carelessly handled. The giant water bugs (*Lethocerus*) of tropical countries are enormous insects, ten cm. long and fierce predators of fish and frogs. In Thailand they command a high price in the markets as a luxury article of diet. There are also aquatic bugs which skate on the tips of their toes over the surface film of the water. Of these the water-striders (*Gerris*) are to be seen on almost any pond.

The land-living Heteroptera are mostly plant feeders, the largest Family of these being the Miridae. They are commonly and confusingly called capsid bugs because the Family comprising them formerly bore the name Capsidae. They are small delicate bugs, often coloured green, and beating foliage into a tray will almost always produce a selection of them. The shield-bugs or stink-bugs (Pentatomidae) are often handsome insects many of which have a shape like a heraldic shield. A few are predators, but most of them feed on sap or fruit juices. Nearly all have a strong unpleasant smell and taste and some display lurid aposematic colours. The Reduviidae or assassin bugs use their powerful beaks for sucking the blood of other insects, larger animals and sometimes of man. They always inject a digestive fluid, and their bite is painful and sometimes very poisonous. The Anthocoridae or flower-bugs are small predators of other insects. They are important in the control of some agricultural pests, and insecticide spraying sometimes has the unfortunate effect of exterminating them and failing to kill their prey, which may then flourish disastrously. There are numerous other Families of Heteroptera which I have not space to mention.

PTERYGOTA: Endopterygota (Holometabola)

21. Mecoptera (300; 4). The small Order of scorpion-flies is a suitable one with which to introduce the Endopterygota, because they are regarded as a little-changed survival of the sort of insects that were the ancestors of most of the Endopterygote Orders. Five of these (numbers 21 to 25 in this catalogue) are associated by entomologists to form a group, the Panorpoid insects. The name is taken from the genus *Panorpa* which includes the commonest scorpion-flies. This conclusion is supported by the fossil record, in which the Mecoptera are well represented in the lower Permian, about 250 million years ago.

A male scorpion-fly, *Panorpa communis*.

Scorpion-flies are usually recognizable by the beak-like head, clear dark-spotted wings and the prominent up-turned genitalia of the male. The fancied resemblance of this feature to a scorpion's sting is the reason for their name. One species, *Panorpa communis*, is often seen in Britain on sunny days along woodland paths. A curious genus called *Boreus*, with vestigial wings, may be found in winter running on damp moss, on which the larva feeds. The larvae of Mecoptera are caterpillar-like with distinct thoracic and abdominal limbs.

22. Neuroptera (4,500; 60). This is a rather diverse Order with a number of Families, but they all have in common membranous wings with complex venation, including a network of cross-veins,

PLATE 19. Large red damselfly (*Pyrrhosoma nymphula*).

PLATE 20. **Hemiptera.** *Above*, a Malaysian cicada, *Platylomia* sp.; *centre*, a shield bug, the forest bug (*Pentatoma rufipes*); *below*, the water cricket (*Velia caprai*), resting on the surface film.

and larvae that are invariably predatory. They are rather different from the other Panorpoid insects, being in some ways more primitive than the Mecoptera. They may represent an early divergence from the Panorpoid stem.

They fall into two well marked suborders. The Megaloptera include the curious long-necked snake-flies *(Rhaphidia)*, whose 'neck' is the elongated prothorax, the alder-flies (Sialidae) and the Corydalidae. The larvae of the last two are aquatic. In North America there are large Corydalids called dobson-flies. These have larvae up to 8 cm. long which live under stones in fast streams, and they are sought out by anglers who use them as bait and call them hellgramites.

Megaloptera larvae have simple biting mouthparts. In the other suborder, the Planipennia, the mandibles and maxillae are coordinated with each other to form a pair of piercing jaws with an open canal running between maxilla and mandible on each side. Through these canals the blood of its prey is sucked by the larva. The Planipennia include the most familiar Neuropterans, the delicate green lacewings, whose golden eyes have given them the Family name Chrysopidae. Almost as common but less conspicuous are the brown lacewings (Hemerobiidae). Lacewing larvae play an important part in the natural control of aphids. Ant-lions (Myrmeleontidae) are found mainly in warm climates. They are named on account of their larvae which make pits in dry dust and lie in wait at the bottom of them, waiting for small wingless insects to slither down their treacherous slopes. Once in the pit an ant is doomed, for the ant-lion baulks its efforts to escape by throwing jets of dust at it; when it finally rolls to the bottom it is seized, killed and sucked dry. The adults fly at night and can be recognized by their short knobbed antennae. The most beautiful of all Neuroptera are the Nemopteridae, which are quite large and have broad fore-wings and long ribbon-like hind-wings. They are found mostly in rather warm, dry countries.

23. Trichoptera (3,000; 188). Caddis-flies are moth-like insects, and are indeed related to the more primitive moths. Their wings are covered with short, fine hairs (not with scales) and their mouthparts are unspecialized and reduced, without functional mandibles. They fly at night and have a characteristic resting attitude with the wings forming a steep V-shaped roof over the back and the antennae laid together and extended forwards. They are more familiar as larvae, the aquatic caddis-worms that make portable cases of various fragmentary materials bound together and lined with silk. The structure of the case and the materials used are usually characteristic of the genus or species. It may consist of short pieces of stick, cut-up segments of leaf, grains of grit or sand or even small shells of water snails. The silk is spun from labial glands just as it is by moth and butterfly larvae. The pupa is formed in the case and has strong mandibles for biting its way out. Some caddis larvae do not make portable cases, but live in silk-lined burrows, and there are predatory species which weave silken nets in flowing water to catch their prey, rather as spiders do on land.

24. Lepidoptera (150,000; 2,200). It is a pity that in English there is no single name to indicate this Order, the laborious formula 'butterflies and moths' being necessary every time it is spoken of. It is an enormous Order, grouped in some eighty Families, of which butterflies comprise six and moths the remainder. Butterflies are mostly large conspicuous insects and fly by day, whereas most moths fly by night and attract less notice, but the distinction between them represents no important division in the natural classification. The two most diagnostic features of the Order are the remarkable coiled proboscis, already described, and the covering of minute overlapping scales on the wings. Each of these is self coloured, but they vary among themselves to an almost infinite degree, and produce intricate and often brilliant patterns on the principle of a mosaic. No other insect Order has evolved such an effective and versatile method of wing coloration, and the wonderful beauty and diversity of butterflies and moths is a product of this. A large number of the examples that I have described of camouflage, warning coloration and mimicry have been taken from the Lepidoptera, simply because they have at their disposal such a great range of adaptive coloration, and have exploited this by also evolving great diversity in wing form and resting posture.

Classification within the Order recognizes about 2 or 3 per cent of them as primitive. The most archaic of all, the tiny Micropterigidae, are so distinct from the rest that they are placed by some authors in a special Order, the **Zeugloptera**, but I will retain this here as a suborder. These are the little dark metallic coloured moths that crowd into buttercups or on rush flowers in early summer. They have fully developed mandibles and feed on pollen.

The common ancestor of the Trichoptera and Lepidoptera may have been similar to these little moths. Among the larger moths the swifts (Hepialidae) are definitely Lepidoptera, but are primitive in some important respects. The most obvious of these concerns the wing venation, which is closely similar in the fore- and hind-wings; it is quite different in all the higher Lepidoptera. The mouthparts of the Hepialids are vestigial and the moths do not feed.

Among the higher Lepidoptera familiar Families are the swallowtail butterflies (Papilionidae), the hawkmoths (Sphingidae) and the emperors and giant silkmoths (Saturniidae), which include the largest insects in the Order. The silkmoth of commerce belongs to another Family, the Bombycidae.

Larvae are usually of the caterpillar type and the great majority feed on leaves and other parts of plants. Some of the blue butterflies (Lycaenidae) have larvae which prey on aphids, and a large number of Lycaenid larvae are more or less closely associated with ants. The ants are attracted by the secretion of a gland on the dorsal surface and may attend the larvae on their food plants or even take them into their nests, where they live by feeding on the ants' larvae and pupae.

The larvae of some small moths (*Plodia* and *Ephestia)* are pests of stored grain, flour, dried fruit and other edible products. Clothes moths probably existed before the age of civilization in old birds' nests and the lairs of carnivorous animals. Some small tropical American moths live only in the fur of live sloths, feeding on the algae that grow on the hairs. When sloths are exterminated by destruction of the forests where they live, these moths will also become extinct.

The pupae of some very primitive small moths, including the Zeugloptera, are exarate, but an obtect pupa, the well known chrysalis, is a characteristic feature of the Order.

25. Diptera (80,000; 5,200). These are the two-winged or 'true' flies whose diagnostic feature is a single pair of wings. The hindwings have become modified to form small stalk- or club-shaped organs called halteres. They vibrate in phase with the wings and serve to control the flight, acting on the same principle as a gyroscope. Artificial breeding of fruitflies (Drosophila) has produced a mutant in which the halteres are replaced by a rudimentary pair of wings.

This is another very large Order of which no detailed account can be given. It falls conveniently into three suborders that show a progression from slender, long-legged types to broad, compact, often bristly flies such as the bluebottle and housefly. The first suborder, the Nematocera, includes crane-flies or daddy-long-legs, gnats and mosquitoes. The intermediate group are the Brachycera, including the big blood-sucking horse-flies and clegs (Tabanidae), the fierce predatory robber-flies (Asilidae) and, in strong contrast to them, the little flower-loving bee-flies (Bombyliidae). The great majority of flies belong to the most advanced suborder, the Cyclorrhapha. All the suborders include species with piercing mouthparts that live by sucking blood, and some of these are vectors of serious diseases such as malaria and yellow fever (mosquitoes) and sleeping sickness (tsetse flies). Some species of this suborder are external parasites of ruminant mammals or of bats.

A crane-fly, *Pedicia rivosa*; this is a large handsome species with patterned wings.

The larvae are the most diverse of any insect Order. The 'leatherjackets' that feed on roots of grass are the larvae of crane-flies. Mosquito larvae are aquatic and swim actively. The only group of flies that can be said to be attractive and useful, the hover-flies (Syrphidae) mostly have flattened, active larvae that live on herbage and prey on aphids. Those of the Muscidae, the house-fly and its numerous relatives, are headless maggots that usually live in decaying or putrid matter, and some of the hover-flies, such as the drone-fly *(Eristalis)* live as larvae in this way. The majority of the tiny flies called Agromyzidae have larvae that are leaf-miners and their mines are very similar to those made by the leaf-mining moths. The larvae of bot-flies and warble-flies are internal parasites of mammals, and I have

PLATE 21. **Trichoptera, Hymenoptera.** *Left*, a caddis-fly, *Stenoplax permistus*; *right*, the hawthorn sawfly (*Trichiosoma lucorum*); *below*, common wasps (*Vespula* sp.) feeding on a fallen apple.

PLATE 22. **Lepidoptera, larger moths.** *Above*, privet hawkmoth (*Sphinx ligustri*); *centre*, pale prominent (*Pterostoma palpina*); *left*, common swift (*Hepialus humili*); *right*, small fanfoot (*Polypogon nemoralis*).

already described the extraordinary breeding habits of some of the Ephydridae.

The pupae are also very diverse. Among the Nematocera the mosquitoes are remarkable in having an actively swimming pupa. In this and the intermediate Order the pupa is nearly always formed in the normal way, by shedding the last larval skin. In the Cyclorrhapha this is retained at pupation to form an oval puparium which protects the pupa just as the silken cocoon of a moth does.

26. Siphonaptera (1,000; 50). The fleas form an isolated Order of wingless external blood-sucking parasites of mammals and birds. As in other parasites most fleas live on a narrow range of hosts, sometimes a single species. It is possible that they are related to the Diptera, or they may be an independent offshoot from the primitive Panorpoid stock. They are rather uniform in structure, flattened from side to side with tough leathery bodies, proof against scratching and preening by the host, and they are also active jumpers. Most of them are permanently active, but the females of the tropical jigger fleas burrow under the host's skin to develop their eggs, swelling to the size of a pea in doing so.

The larvae do not live on the host's body but in the dust and debris of its nest or lair. They feed on the organic dust of feathers, fur or wool and also, it is believed, on dried blood that the adult fleas provide by sucking far more than they need and voiding it undigested. Their larval habits limit fleas to parasitizing animals that have a nest or lair to which they repeatedly return. Domestic cats, dogs, pigs, many rodents and men come into this category, as well as a great many birds. Ruminant mammals and non-human primates, such as monkeys, are free of fleas. Some of them are carriers of disease and are associated with plague in men and rodents and with myxomatosis in rabbits.

27. Hymenoptera (100,000; 6,100). This Order comprises the wasps, bees, ants and ichneumons, and the less familiar sawflies and wood-wasps. They have one constant feature: the wings are connected by a row of minute hooks on the hind-wing which engage in a fold on the hind margin of the fore-wing. Also the anterior segment of the abdomen is fused to the thorax. Together with the Lepidoptera and Diptera they are among the more recently evolved insects; the main evolutionary development of these three Orders probably accompanied that of the flowering plants during the past 80 to 100 million years. The Hymenoptera are described on their own because their affinities with other insects have not been determined with any certainty. All four wings are normally present, but their venation is difficult to correlate with the basic pattern to which all the hitherto described winged Orders more or less conform.

There is also a pattern of behaviour which runs right through the Order, that of increasingly elaborate provision by the females for the larvae which will hatch from their eggs. This ranges from simple implanting of the eggs in an edible medium suited to their particular needs, through the provision of food stores by the solitary wasps and bees to the meticulous nursing of the larvae and pupae by the social Hymenoptera, which are regarded as the most highly evolved of all insects.

Two well marked suborders are recognized. The more primitive one, the Symphyta, includes the sawflies and wood-wasps. They are distinguished from the higher Hymenoptera by having no 'wasp waist'. Female sawflies have a blade-like ovipositor that is usually armed with teeth like a saw, and they cut slits in stems and leaves into which the eggs are inserted. Their larvae usually feed on plants and are curiously like those of the Lepidoptera, but have a larger number of abdominal feet. The big *Urocerus* (formerly *Sirex*) *gigas* is a typical wood-wasp. Here the ovipositor is used to bore into the living wood of trees, and the larvae of *U. gigas* may do serious damage by boring in pine trunks.

In the far larger suborder Apocrita the part of the abdomen just behind the thorax is constricted to form a waist, which is remarkably slender in some wasps. Bees, ants, the parasitic ichneumon wasps and some minute gall-wasps are included in this suborder, which is divided into about a dozen superfamilies. These fall into two groups, the 'Aculeata' and the 'Parasitica', but the division between them is not clear-cut, and they are not recognized as taxonomic categories. The former usually have a sting (wasps, bees, ants) and the latter lead a parasitic life as larvae. Most of the Aculeata make habitations or nests which they stock with food for their larvae, or which are inhabited by a few fully sexed individuals and populations of sterile females which nurse the larvae as well as gathering food for them and defending the nest with their stings. Most species of wasps and bees are 'solitary', each female making and stocking her own nest; a minority of them, and all ants, are social insects.

28. Coleoptera (278,000; 3,700). Last but not least the beetles. This is by far the largest Order in the Animal Kingdom; one in four of all the animal species described and named is a beetle. It is quite possible that there are twice or three times as many species of beetles in existence as are now known to science. Of course they will never all be described, many will be exterminated before they can be discovered.

Few generalizations can be made about them. They all have the mandibles developed, and elaborate modification of the mouthparts is rare though feeding habits vary greatly. Though most of them can fly there is a larger proportion of flightless species than in any other Order of insects that are normally winged. One gets an impression that beetles are at home where they can get a foothold, on the ground or on vegetation, not in the air as dragonflies, flies or butterflies are. This way of life is associated with the very general development of armour. In a typical beetle the fore-wings are modified to form a pair of curved shields which completely cover the hind-wings and the abdomen, and the under surface is also protected by sclerotized body segments rigidly welded together. One can suppose that the extra weight of all this armour plate can be accepted by an insect that is airborne only for short periods. In one very large Family, the Staphylinidae, the wing-covers or elytra are short and do not extend back over the abdomen, so that the beetles look rather like earwigs; the devil's coach-horse is an example of them. However the elytra are developed the hind-wings are folded beneath them in a complicated manner when the beetle is not flying. In many flightless species the elytra are welded in the middle line and quite immovable. The most aberrant of all are the Stylopoidea, in which the females are internal parasites of other insects. In the males the hind-wings are large and fan-like and the elytra are reduced to little knobs, resembling the halteres of

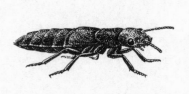

The devil's coach-horse beetle, at rest and (*right*) in its threatening posture.

flies. Until recently the Stylopoidea have been treated as a separate Order called the Strepsiptera.

Beetle larvae vary according to their mode of life and there is a gradation from active predatory types with well developed antennae, mouthparts and legs to 'grubs' that burrow in wood or are otherwise surrounded by their food supply. The pupa is usually exarate, with the appendages free and movable, but ladybirds and a few other beetles have obtect pupae.

The beetles' affinities with other insects are obscure. They were already in existence in the Permian period, 280 to 225 million years ago, when most of the insect Orders were in an early stage of evolution and some had not yet appeared. Classification divides them into two main suborders, the Adephaga and Polyphaga. The first means 'ravenous eaters' and the second, in free translation, 'eaters of almost everything'. The Adephaga include the predatory ground beetles (Carabidae), the tiger beetles and also most of the predatory water beetles such as the well-known *Dytiscus*. About 150 Families are included in the Polyphaga: familiar ones are the rove-beetles (Staphylinidae), stag-beetles (Lucanidae), chafers and dung-beetles (Scarabaeidae), jewel beetles (Buprestidae), click-beetles (Elateridae), ladybirds (Coccinellidae), longhorns or longicorns (Cerambycidae) and weevils (Curculionidae).

CHAPTER 5

MAN AND INSECTS

THE HISTORY OF ENTOMOLOGY

It is interesting to compare man's conscious relationship with insects today with that of 300 years ago. During the 17th century the very first intelligible descriptions of such obvious insects as butterflies appeared in England. They were written in Latin and so noticed by only a tiny minority who were both educated and eccentric enough to be naturalists. The only insects known to the average townsman were flies and the species that he found hopping and crawling about his person. In the country the 'butter-coloured fly' that we now call the brimstone or *Gonepteryx rhamni* appeared as a welcome harbinger of spring, and its name, contracted and used more comprehensively, is still with us; other butterflies seem to have been disregarded. There were wasps that stung, flies that tormented cattle, bees (which were still confused with hoverflies), beetles, dragonflies and a few other conspicuous insects that received a sort of broad, vague recognition. Very few people enquired into their diversity or their habits because no advantage was apparent and no credit was gained by doing so. The notion that there were tens of thousands of species of insects was as far from men's minds as electric light or telephones.

The reproduction of the higher animals and man was fairly well comprehended, but creatures at the level of insects were not understood to be limited in the same way. It was believed without question that they might be generated from mud or putrefying matter, or simply from the soil, without any sort of parental process; the 'animalculae', protozoans and the like, revealed in tainted water by the early microscopes, were regarded as being of spontaneous generation well into the 19th century.

All living things were believed to have been created, together with man, at the same time, man being the Lord of Creation with the rest of nature ordered solely for his well being. Even now this idea lingers, and one hears empty-headed questions like 'what is the use of a beetle?' Obviously hostile phenomena such as visitations of locusts were sent to remind us of our sins and persuade us to turn away from them. Only a hundred years ago this curiously primitive dogma was invoked in the State of Missouri to give active discouragement to the brilliant founder of economic entomology C. V. Riley, who was striving to organize practical measures against the scourge of the Rocky Mountain locust.

The invention by Linnaeus in the mid-18th century of a workable system of naming animals and plants gave a tremendous stimulus to enquiry in all branches of zoology, entomology included. Publication in 1758 of the tenth edition of his *Systema Naturae* set an example that enabled naturalists who could never meet, and who spoke different languages, to coordinate their discoveries intelligibly. The general use of Latin as a means of communication is now virtually confined to biological nomenclature. Failure to maintain its use as a language is the one great loss that science and culture have suffered during the last couple of centuries. If it had been retained people inclined towards learning and travel would have had to learn one language in addition to their own to enable them to go about the world largely unimpeded by the curse of Babel.

INSECTS AND HEALTH

Linnaeus gave biology its most important instrument. Just a hundred years later Darwin provided a philosophy through which we can understand how and why life on earth came to be ordered as it is. Not long after the publication of *The Origin of Species* the importance of insects to our health began to be realized. In 1878 Patrick Manson showed that the filaria worms that cause elephantiasis are carried by mosquitoes. The association of these insects with malaria and yellow fever came at about the turn of the century. These insects had always been enemies of man and achieved the status of 'pests' through recognition of their part in spreading disease. It must not be forgotten that this recognition would not have been possible without the basis of entomological science that had been built up in the earlier 1800's by unpractical and often derided bug-hunters.

PESTS AND PEST CONTROL

At various times in the 19th century examples of another type of insect pest appeared, a type which men created from perfectly harmless species by his huge scale interference with the natural environment. The Colorado potato beetle affords a good example. It was first discovered in 1823 in the upper Missouri River region of the Rocky Mountains. It was feeding on the buffalo burr, a plant of the nightshade Family, to which the potato also belongs. It is a pretty insect and at that time was no doubt regarded as a rarity from a little known region and something of an entomological prize. Unfortunately the leaves of buffalo burr and potato have a similar taste. When the American West became settled and potato culture was introduced there the beetle transferred to it and multiplied. It became a pest of potato simply because men covered square miles of ground with potato plants, creating an environment like nothing in nature, and nothing like the small-scale mixed agriculture of even highly civilized men up to about 150 years ago. The Colorado beetle reached the Atlantic coast in 1874. By 1920 it had got into a ship's cargo of some kind and established itself in France, and now it is found all over Europe from Spain to western Russia. There have been outbreaks in Britain but the beetle is not established here and a constant watch is kept for it. In the harsh and changeable weather of the Rockies it acquired a remarkably wide tolerance for climate. It thrives in the desert country of Texas and survives the intensely cold winters of Canada and central Europe. It can probably live wherever man can grow potatoes.

Increase in speed and ease of communications all over the world has resulted again and again in the accidental transport of insect species from their home territories to other regions with a climate in which they can live. As a result insects that feed on widely cultivated crop plants may become far more serious pests than they are at home. The usual reason for this is that their natural enemies, especially parasitoids, almost invariably fail to accompany them, so that these important checks on their increase do not operate. The small white or cabbage white butterfly *(Pieris rapae)* is an example of this. It is a native of Europe and temperate Asia, where it is a nuisance when its larvae attack brassica vegetables. It first reached North America about 1860 and has spread over most of the continent. In 1930 it appeared in New Zealand and, probably from there, reached southern Australia and Tasmania in 1939 to 1940. In New Zealand and Australia it rapidly became a serious pest because no allied butterflies occur there, so none of the local parasitoids were adapted to attack it. In New Zealand introduction from England of the Chalcid wasp *Pteromalus puparum* quickly reduced the numbers of the butterfly, and both this and two species of *Apanteles* have been released in Australia with good results. The parasitoids can be given the same advantage as that initially enjoyed by pests of exotic origin, by taking great care to avoid introducing any of the relevant hyperparasitic species. Most successful essays in biological control have this pattern. Towards the end of the last century the cottony-cushion scale insect accidentally found its way from Australia to the California citrus orchards and devastated them. In 1889 an Australian ladybird beetle, *Rhodalia cardinalis,* was introduced and quickly brought the pest under control. A final example of a slightly different kind concerns the prickly pear cactus, introduced into Australia as an ornamental plant early in this century. In the 1920's it ran wild in Queensland and New South Wales and covered millions of acres of grazing land with an impenetrable jungle of spines. After a long search in America for suitable cactus-feeding insects a small Argentinian moth, *Cactoblastis cactorum,* was released in the infested country, and the prickly pear simply melted away under the swarming hordes of its larvae; it was estimated that 22 million acres of useful land was reclaimed.

Biological control of this kind is usually only practical against insects that have colonized new territories, leaving their natural enemies behind; even then it is not always successful. Far more reliance is placed on chemical biocides, a biocide being by definition a destroyer of life. Starting two centuries ago with nicotine and pyrethrum, sprays and powders were elaborated and used with rather meagre success up to about 1940. In the years following this there was a sensational breakthrough with various synthetic insecticides, the best known being the chlorinated hydrocarbons which include DDT, aldrin and dieldrin.

The story of these, told in Rachel Carson's book *Silent Spring* and innumerable subsequent publications arguing on both sides, is too well known to need any recapitulation. Residues of these biocides are present in the bodies of practically everyone. In small concentrations they are not known to be harmful, but it cannot be stated that they are harmless because no one has yet lived a normal lifetime in the environment they have created. In large concentrations they are deadly, not only to insects but to vertebrate animals as well. Wild life has been extensively destroyed and they are so universal that traces of these biocides are present in the bodies of Antarctic penguins.

The risk to human health and the hazard to wild life has led to the

PLATE 23. **Lepidoptera, smaller moths.** *Above left*, brown chinamark (*Nymphula nympheata*); *right*, grass-moth, *Agriphila tristella*; *below left*, Tortricid moth, *Lozotaenia forsterana*; *right*, plume moth, *Emmelina monodactyla*.

PLATE 24. **Beetles.** *Left*, a weevil, *Balaninus venosus*; *right*, *Lathrobium multipunctatum* (Staphylinidae); *below*, door beetle (*Geotrupes* sp.).

banning of DDT in some countries and to a general awareness of
the dangers of trying to exterminate insects by disseminating
poison. The lesson we must all accept is that total warfare,
whether waged against insects or against our fellow men, endan-
gers not only the enemy but the attacker as well, and everything
living on the earth.

DOMESTICATED INSECTS

The destruction of weeds or other insects is not the only use to
which man can put insect species. Two of them have a history of
domestication nearly as long as that of dogs and horses; they are of
course the honeybee and the silkworm. Both merit chapters or
whole books to themselves, but I shall only remark on one conspicuous difference between them which seldom receives any
emphatic notice. The silk-moth *(Bombyx mori)* is an utterly docile
insect in both its active stages. The larvae need no caging but will
feed on their mulberry leaves in open trays without wandering
away, and the moths, though fully winged, seldom fly, the females
never. No wild ancestor of the silk-moth is known. Almost certainly it lived in China, but selective breeding of the captive
insects, conducted on a huge scale for hundreds of years, produced
strains so devoid of the patterns of behaviour necessary for survival in the wild that they could not possibly maintain themselves if
they were liberated or escaped. What the escaping moths could
and undoubtedly did do was to mate with those of the wild stock,
contaminating it with their artificially selected genes of helpless
inactivity and gradually reducing its viability. Continued over
centuries there can be little doubt that this process led to the
extinction of *Bombyx mori* in the wild.

Now look at the honeybee. Until very recent times selective
breeding of this insect has been impossible because the marriage
flight of the queens and drones cannot be controlled. *Apis mellifera*
remains a wholly efficient wild animal, and a swarm from a hive
can establish itself in a hollow tree and live there just as it did
before *Homo sapiens* had evolved from his pre-human ancestors.
A delicate technique of artificial insemination has now been
devised for bees and has been going on for some time. As they must
fly freely to gather nectar and carry pollen honeybees will never be
degraded to the level of silk-moths, but we shall change and tame
them.

Domesticated bees are now more important as pollinators than they are as producers of honey. There are, however, some economically important plants which are better served by wild bees, two of them being clover and lucerne or alfalfa. Bumblebees are essential if clover is to produce seed, and the best pollinators of lucerne are certain small solitary species, as already mentioned on p.103. In the U.S.A. natural breeding of these bees is severely inhibited by settlement, intensive agriculture and the use of pesticides, and it was found that lucerne only set seed satisfactorily in newly cultivated areas.

The pioneer in solving this problem was Dr W. P. Stephen. Working in Oregon he found that the alkali bee *(Nomia melanderi)* was an effective pollinator. It nests in burrows in the soil and is gregarious, occupying areas where the soil is both moist and devoid of thick vegetation due to salt-laden water overlying an impervious hardpan. Such places are wholly altered and destroyed by ploughing or any other disturbance, so Dr Stephen prepared elaborate bee beds, carefully provided with adequate moisture and drainage and enough salt to simulate the alkaline soil that the bees naturally seek. Blocks of soil from natural bee beds, transplanted in spring and containing large numbers of overwintering larvae, were inserted into the artificial beds. When the female bees hatch and mate their gregarious instinct leads them to continue breeding in the same place, digging their burrows so close together that populations of between one and two thousand nesting females per square metre can be maintained. The combined effect of these artificial bee beds and conservation of natural sites in Oregon resulted in yields of alfalfa seed up to 2,000 pounds per acre, a ten-fold increase over the average for the preceding ten years.

Accidental introduction of insects from Europe to America has usually been unfortunate, but the small leaf-cutter bee *Megachile rotundata* provides a happy exception to this. No one knows when it arrived, but it was observed to be another effective pollinator of lucerne, and can easily be provided with artificial accommodation. Its natural nesting sites are small holes and crevices, which are lined with pieces of leaf in the usual fashion of leaf-cutter bees. It is now cultured in the U.S.A. and Canada on a scale that amounts to a minor industry. It is a small bee and at first bundles of drinking straws were provided for it to nest in, but now far more elaborate batteries of tubes are made, that can be opened up, cleaned and re-used, and measures are taken to protect the bees from the numerous parasites that beset them in nature. As it does not fly as far as the alkali bee when foraging, little houses or shelters are made, each containing several thousand nesting tubes, and these are placed at intervals in the alfalfa fields. *M. rotundata* cannot survive the Canadian winter in the open, and so large stocks of cocoons are transferred indoors at the end of the summer and the hatching bees are released in the spring.

Bees are not the only recently enlisted allies of man. Ever since cattle farming became a large-scale activity in Australia it has had to cope with a peculiar and little publicized problem, that of the cow-pat. Each one of these deposits covers a definite area of ground, and it also stimulates a surrounding growth of rank grass which cattle dislike, so that there is a large aggregate loss in the total area of pasture. In 1966 this was estimated at 300,000 acres (over 120,000 hectares) representing an annual loss of £2.33 million for the year. The dung also provides a breeding ground for flies and harmful parasitic worms.

In any other part of the world all this dung would have been put underground by Scarabaeid beetles almost as fast as it accumulated, but Australian dung beetles, conditioned to the relatively dry and meagre droppings of kangaroos, disregard cow-pats entirely. During the past few years a project on the biological control of cattle dung has been in progress. African and Mexican dung-beetles have been released and at least one is well established in Queensland. Different species are required for acclimatization in various parts of Australia, and work on the problem is continuing. Not only is this a lesson in how to make good use of insects, it also emphasizes the enormously valuable service done by dung-beetles in parts of the world where they are indigenous and numerous. Not only cattle dung but human excrement by hundreds of tons is put tidily and hygienically underground in hot countries where sophisticated disposal of sewage is not yet available.

The small beetle *Trilobium confusum* is a pest of stored meal and flour, but it can render service to us as well. In Canada, where new strains of cereals are constantly produced at agricultural research stations, the nutritional value of hybrid grain is tested by giving it to larvae of this beetle. If they grow to full size rapidly the strain is worth persisting with; if not it must be modified or abandoned. The short life cycle of *Trilobium* enables testing to be carried out quickly and research is speeded up accordingly.

Ever since genetics developed into an experimental science

insects have been of the greatest value in its pursuit. The principle of sex linkage of genes was first recognized in the course of breeding varieties of the magpie moth, and the most important animal used in experiments on heredity is the tiny fruit-fly, *Drosophila*. They are easy to breed, complete their life cycle rapidly and mutations frequently occur among them. Also they have only four chromosomes in the cell nucleus, an abnormally low number which simplifies work on them, and the chromosomes in the salivary glands are unusually large, making ideal material for microscopic study.

STUDYING INSECTS

Insects do not only minister to our material and scientific needs, many of them are wonderful and beautiful. Learn a little about the large day fliers, butterflies and dragonflies, and you will find that watching them is just as rewarding as watching birds. Many smaller insects are exquisite if closely examined. To do this one must generally collect and preserve them, and a great deal of aesthetic and intellectual pleasure can be derived from collecting. There are circumstances under which this may endanger insect populations, and it should never be aimed at species which are recognized as being in need of protection, nor, of course, pursued in nature reserves unless permission for research has been obtained. If strict attention is paid to these principles and only small numbers of each species are taken, collecting, by stimulating interest, does more good than harm in terms of conservation.

The hunting and killing of insects for commercial ends, to provide material for sale as ornaments, should be condemned and discouraged in every way. Large insects with relatively low population numbers are nearly always selected, and there is no limit to the number that the hunter will catch and kill in the hope of selling them to dealers.

Photography affords another approach to insects from which a great deal of pleasure can be derived. A good single-lens reflex camera is needed, with a few accessories for close-up work, and the use of electronic flash is of so much assistance in getting good results that I regard it as essential. Most recent books on nature photography have enough information to give the beginner a start, but you will not achieve first class results without a bit of experience. Photographing butterflies in the field is harder work than catching them, but when you have mastered the use of your equipment you can bring home pictures of the living insects on which the rows of scales on the wings are clearly shown, much better trophies than pinned specimens. To a casual glance, a small beetle may appear as little more than a moving green, blue or red spot; photograph it successfully and you can throw on the screen an image of a resplendent creature covered in jointed armour more polished and intricately articulated than that of a mediaeval fighting king. To photograph a bird or mammal species for the first time you must now travel far afield indeed, but there are likely to be insects in your garden of which no one has ever taken a photograph.

Conservation of wild life is now fully recognized as a present need and an obligation to future generations. Its application to insects has not captured public imagination to any great extent, but the butterflies of our countryside give delight to just as many people as do the badgers and otters. In New Guinea the birds of paradise and the great birdwing swallowtails fly together and the loss of either would be equally disastrous.

Destruction of habitat far outweighs hunting and collecting as a factor in exterminating animal life of all kinds, and this applies equally to the brutal massacre of the tropical rain forest and to the greedy compulsive tidiness of mechanized agriculture in our own countryside and everywhere else. It is heartening to reflect that nature reserves and other measures advertised as beneficial to birds and mammals usually promote the well being of a host of insects as well. But remember too that insect populations can thrive in quite small areas in which the right type of vegetation is allowed to grow. An acre of reeds standing in shallow water, a fairly extensive bramble thicket, a mile of a wide road verge cut back no further than it need be, a patch of nettles in the corner of your garden: any wilderness, however small, is worth preserving. Above all, the more people who appreciate the wonder and beauty of insect life the easier it is to promote means to preserve it.

BOOKS TO READ

General introductions to entomology

EVANS, H. E. (1970). *Life on a Little-known Planet*. Andre Deutsch. A series of most informative and entertaining essays on insect life.

FORD, R. L. E. (1973). *Studying Insects*. Frederick Warne. A useful summary of methods of collecting, preserving and breeding insects.

IMMS, A. D. (1959). *Outlines of Entomology*. Methuen & Co. The best short formal introduction.

IMMS, A. D. (1971). *Insect Natural History*. Collins New Naturalist. An excellent account of the biology of British insects.

KLOTS, A. B. and KLOTS, E. B. (1959). *Living Insects of the World*. Hamish Hamilton. A good and well illustrated survey of the insect Orders on a world basis.

WIGGLESWORTH, V. B. (1964). *The Life of Insects*. Weidenfeld & Nicolson. A readable and well illustrated book on insect biology.

Accounts of particular groups or subjects

BUTLER, COLIN G. (1975). *The World of the Honeybee*. Collins New Naturalist. A detailed natural history of one species of insect.

COLYER, C. N. and HAMMOND, O. C. (1951). *Flies of the British Isles*. Frederick Warne. A well presented and illustrated introduction to a very large subject.

CORBET, P. S., LONGFIELD, C. and MOORE, N. W. (1960). *Dragonflies*. Collins New Naturalist. A complete and well illustrated account of the British species.

EVANS, G. (1975). *The Life of Beetles*. George Allen & Unwin. An up-to-date biology of beetles on a world-wide basis.

EVANS, H. E. and EBERHARD, M. J. W. (1970). *The Wasps*. David & Charles. A readable and informative account of its subject.

FORD, E. B. (1957). *Butterflies*. Collins New Naturalist. The biology of British butterflies, with emphasis on genetics.

FORD, E. B. (1972). *Moths*. Collins New Naturalist. A similar approach to *Butterflies* but necessarily not comprehensive and confined to the larger moths.

FREE, J. B. and BUTLER, C. G. (1959). *Bumblebees*. Collins New Naturalist. A natural history of all the British species.

PROCTOR, M. and YEO, P. (1973). *The Pollination of Flowers*. Collins New Naturalist. A unique monograph of the subject and a book for botanists and entomologists alike.

SKAIFE, S. H. (1955). *Dwellers in Darkness*. Longmans Green. An interesting study of termites based on a South African species.

WILLIAMS, C. B. (1958). *Insect Migration*. Collins New Naturalist. The best introduction to a rather mysterious branch of entomology.

Identification of British and European insects

BEIRNE, B. P. (1952). *British Pyralid and Plume Moths*. Frederick Warne. Deals with two Families of the 'Microlepidoptera'.

BURTON, J. (1968). *The Oxford Book of Insects*. Oxford University Press. A well selected and well illustrated survey of British insects.

CHINERY, M. (1973). *A Field Guide to the Insects of Britain and Europe*. Collins. A well presented introduction with the emphasis on northern Europe.

HEATH, J., Editor (Vol 1, 1976). *The Moths and Butterflies of Great Britain and Ireland*. Blackwell Scientific Publications & Curwen Press. In course of publication; one volume has appeared. All the British Lepidoptera are to be included.

HIGGINS, L. G. and RILEY, N. D. (1975). *A Field Guide to the Butterflies of Britain and Europe*. Collins. All the species systematically described and illustrated.

HOWARTH, T. G. (1973). *South's British Butterflies*, Frederick Warne. A much enlarged and revised version of the early butterfly book by Richard South. Varieties and life histories all illustrated in colour.

LINNSEN, E. F. (1959). *Beetles of the British Isles*, Vols 1 and 2. The emphasis is on identification, but only a selection of species is described and illustrated.

RAGGE, D. R. (1965). *Grasshoppers, Crickets and Cockroaches of the British Isles*. Frederick Warne. Provides for identification of all the species and gives a good account of their natural history.

SOUTH, R. (1961). *The Moths of the British Isles*, Vols 1 and 2. Frederick Warne. Provides for identification of the 'macrolepidoptera'. In need of revision.

SOUTHWOOD, T. R. E. and LESTON, D. (1959). *Land and Water Bugs of the British Isles*. Frederick Warne. Heteroptera only. Contains a great deal of biological information besides plates and keys for identification.

STEP, E. (1932). *Bees, Wasps, Ants and allied Insects of the British Isles*. Frederick Warne. Nomenclature out of date, but a good informative book.

GLOSSARY

Page references are to discussion or fuller definitions

Aorta: the main dorsal blood vessel.

Aposematic: term describing colour, form or behaviour that serves as a warning of distasteful or dangerous properties.

Apterygota: the primitively wingless insects (p. 144).

Arthropoda: one of the major divisions of the Animal Kingdom (p. 11).

Biomass: the aggregate mass or weight of an assemblage or population of animals.

Cercus: one of a pair of appendages at the tip of the abdomen (p. 12).

Chitin: the tough fibrous basis of the cuticle or outer covering of insects (p. 16).

Chromosomes: thread-like bodies in the nuclei of living cells, which carry the hereditary genes.

Class: the taxonomic category between Phylum and Order (p. 142).

Coprophagous: feeding on dung.

Coxa: the basal joint of the leg (p. 13).

Cuticle: the outer covering or 'skin' of an insect.

Ecdysis: the act of moulting in an arthropod.

Ectoparasite: a parasite that lives on the outside of the host's body.

Endemic: indigenous to a locality or region and wholly confined to it.

Endopterygota: the more highly evolved winged insects (p. 55).

Epicuticle: the waterproof waxy layer covering the cuticle in insects.

Exopterygota: the more primitive winged insects (p. 55).

Exotic: originating from another territory, not indigenous; in Australia the rabbit is an exotic animal, the platypus is not.

Family: the taxonomic category between Order and genus (p. 142).

Femur: the third and usually largest joint of the leg (p. 13).

Fibrillar muscle: a type of muscle that can contract without needing a nervous impulse as stimulation (p. 24).

Galea: the outer lobe of the maxilla (p. 13).

Ganglion: a central mass of nerve cells.

Gene: a single hereditary unit, one of many carried on a chromosome.

Genus: a taxonomic assemblage of closely related species (p. 142).

Honey: a sweet substance made from nectar by bees.

Honeydew: a sugary excretion of bugs of the suborder Homoptera.

Hyperparasite: a parasite of a parasite; commonest among parasitoids.

Imago: the adult or final instar of an insect (p. 55).

Indigenous: occurring as part of the natural fauna of a locality or region, but not necessarily confined to it.

Instar: the form assumed by an insect during a particular stadium (p. 55).

Labial palp: an appendage of the labium (p. 13).

Labium: the lower lip (p. 13).

Labrum: the upper lip (p. 13).

Lacinia: the inner lobe of the maxilla (p. 13).

Larva: the succession of instars, during which an insect feeds and grows, before the pupal instar (p. 55).

Lepidopterist: a student or collector of butterflies and moths.

Malpighian tubules: tubular excretory organs (p. 12).

Mandibles: the jaws (p. 13).

Maxillae: paired mouth appendages (p. 13).

Maxillary palp: an appendage of the maxilla (p. 13).

Mesothorax: the middle segment of the thorax.

Metamorphosis: changes undergone in the course of an animal's growth.

Metathorax: the hind segment of the thorax.

Mimicry: the resemblance, supposed to afford protection, of an edible or harmless animal to one which is distasteful or dangerous; resemblance to leaves, twigs etc. is not mimicry but procrypsis.

Nectar: a sweet secretion produced by flowers to attract insects.

Nymph: the pre-adult stages of insects without a pupal instar (p. 55).

Ocelli: simple eyes (p. 31).

Oesophagus: the gullet.

Ommatidium: a unit of the compound eye of an insect (p. 32).

Order: the taxonomic category between Class and Family (p. 142).

Paranota: paired lobes on the thoracic segments of primitive insects from which the wings are believed to have been evolved.

Parasitoid: a parasite whose life cycle always involves the death of its host (p. 110).

Parthenogenesis: reproduction without fertilization of the egg or ovum.

Pheromone: a secretion of definite chemical composition whose usual purpose is olfactory communication between members of a species.

Phylum: the largest taxonomic category within the Animal Kingdom.

Pupa: the instar between the last larval stadium and the imago (p. 55).

Procrypsis (or Crypsis): adaptation to render an animal inconspicuous; protective camouflage.

Prothorax: the front segment of the thorax.

Protozoa: the most primitive phylum of the Animal Kingdom, comprising single-celled or non-cellular animals.

Resilin: an elastic substance that forms part of the mechanism of jumping and of wing action in insects (p. 19).

Reticulate: like a net.

Retinula: the structure formed of light-sensitive cells which surrounds the rhabdom in compound eyes (p. 32).

Rhabdom: the central rod of the ommatidium in compound eyes, surrounded by the retinula (p. 32).

Sclerotin: a horny substance, derived from chitin, of which the hard parts of insects are formed (p. 16).

Sclerotized: formed of sclerotin.

Species: a particular 'kind' of animal or plant; the population comprising a species can breed freely among themselves.

Spiracles: external openings of the breathing system of insects (p. 15).

Stadium: the interval between two ecdyses (p. 54).

Stridulation: production of sound by scraping or rubbing together of modified surfaces.

Symbiosis: an association of living creatures which operates for their mutual benefit.

Tarsus: a series of small segments making up the foot of an insect (p. 13).

Taxonomy: the science of classifying and naming living things.

Thorax: the three segments of an insect behind the head, which bear the three pairs of legs and two of wings.

Tibia: the shank of the leg (p 13).

Tracheae: the fine tubes by means of which insects breathe (p. 15).

Trochanter: a small joint of the leg (p 13).

Tympanum: ear drum.

Zoogeography: the study of the geographical distribution of animals as determined by their evolutionary history.

INDEX